THE ADEPT

THE ADEPT

Selections from Talks and Essays by DA FREE JOHN
on the Nature and Function of the Enlightened Teacher

*Compiled and Edited with Introduction and Commentary
by Georg Feuerstein, Ty Koontz, and David Dykstra*

The Dawn Horse Press
Clearlake, California

Copyright © The Johannine Daist Communion 1983. All rights reserved. No part of this book may be used or reproduced in any manner without written permission except in the case of brief quotations embodied in critical articles or reviews.

First edition July 1983
Printed in the United States of America
International Standard Book Number: paper 0-913922-81-1

Produced by The Johannine Daist Communion
in cooperation with The Dawn Horse Press

CONTENTS

Introduction   9

PART ONE
The Nature and Work of the Adept

I	**Guru Is a Function**	**17**
	The Urgency of the Adept's Work	17
	The Adept Is the Source of Religious Life	19
	The Superphysics of Spiritual Evolution	22
	The Guru Is a Sacrifice	25
	The Paradox of the Divine Person	30
II	**The Right Approach to the Adept**	**33**
	The Adept Is Not a Cultic Idol	33
	The Adept Is a Demand	37
III	**The Radical Relationship**	**42**
	The Relationship to the Adept Transcends the Verbal Teaching	42
	Devotion to the Guru	47
	The Devotee Does Not Choose the Adept	51
	The Guru Enters the Devotee	52
	The Devotee Is Necessary for the Guru's Work	55
IV	**Crazy Wisdom**	**60**

PART TWO

The Adept Da Free John and His Compassionate Work

V	Biographical Confessions	67
	The Early Life	67
	The Teaching Work	71
	The Hermitage Phase and Universal Blessing	74
	After the Death of the Adept	77
VI	The Divine Person	79
	The Adept Is the Unborn Reality	79
	"I Am You"	82
	The Accomplishing Power	84
VII	The Devotee's Response	87
	Only Understanding Avails	87
	"Come to Me When You Are Already Happy"	89

EPILOGUE

What Will You Do If You Love Me?   93

Appendix: The Seven Stages of Life	97
About The Johannine Daist Communion	104
An Invitation	104
The Books of Master Da Free John	105

The Perfect Teachers of Man are the Transcendental Adepts. They appear in various times and places, to Awaken all individual beings to the Living Divine and to create a renewal of truly human and spiritual culture. They unanimously declare and confess that only the Living God, the Eternally Radiant Divine Being in whom all beings and things arise and inhere, is the Truth and Ever-Present Savior of Man. The Adepts come and go. They Serve and Incarnate the One who is always already here.

> Da Free John
> *Scientific Proof of the Existence of God Will Soon Be Announced by the White House!*

INTRODUCTION

"Adept" is a word that is not prominent in the daily vocabulary of most people. If it is used at all, it is generally employed as an adjective, in the sense of "experienced" or "skilled." As a noun, the word is largely confined to more scholarly contexts, where it denotes an initiate of an esoteric tradition or teaching. Neither of these two principal connotations quite applies to the way in which the term is used on the following pages, even though there is a definite overlap.

The Adept, as understood here, is one who has transcended all of the limitations normally considered to be inevitable in human life. Notably, he has gone beyond the mistaken identification with the body-mind as it is ordinarily experienced. He knows it to be markedly different from the way it is commonly understood, and therefore he also relates to it differently. He is irrevocably certain that the body is more than the visible male or female organism and that, together with the mind, it is a multidimensional reality within an equally multidimensional and paradoxical universe. This he knows to be the case from firsthand "experience," or rather from a Realization that transcends experience, and not merely as a matter of opinion or belief.

He shares this "experience" with the conventional mystic, yogi, or sage. Where he goes beyond their spiritual realization and comprehension of reality is in his utter and permanent transcendence of the ego. In other words, the Adept has altogether ceased to identify with the body-mind or any of the phenomena associated with it. He is Conscious as the identity of the Total Field of Being. He *is* all there is. He is an initiate not of any esoteric school, but of the Mystery of existence itself.

His Condition must not be confused with any altered state of awareness or mystical attainment, which are only temporary changes in the quality of the body-mind (in its wider sense). He does not, strictly, experience anything, because all phenomena, including the body-mind with which he was previously associated through an act of (mistaken) identification, simply arise in the Expanse of the Being that he is.

This is a brainteaser and difficult even to picture, which is part of the problem of communicating the Adept's Realization. It does not make much logical sense. As with some of the findings of quantum physics, one can perhaps have an intuitive sense of this Condition, but even then the mind is baffled by its paradoxical nature. For, how can one be conscious of anything if there is no ego or subjective center of experience? This question only poses itself by virtue of the widespread misconception of the nature of consciousness. According to the current (materialist) interpretation of human existence, consciousness is a brain phenomenon, a firing of the cerebral synapses. In this view, it gets snuffed out the moment the brain cells die. But apart from being an obviously unwarranted reduction of mental processes to biochemical activity, this theory deals not with consciousness but only with the contents of consciousness. This is, in fact, all that science can ever hope to analyze or attempt to understand. For, consciousness is the Transcendental Witness, or Being-Consciousness, that does not undergo any modification and that is the Universal Matrix of all changing conditions pertaining to the manifest realm of existence.

This is the unequivocal message of the long history of mysticism and the authoritative testimony of the great Adepts of humanity. Eliot Deutsch, professor of philosophy and longstanding researcher into Eastern traditions, suggests that there are two primary modes of consciousness—the "bound" or personal consciousness and the "boundless" or universal consciousness which is here styled the Transcendental Consciousness.

> Consciousness is bound whenever it is in virtue of its objects. ('My') consciousness is bound whenever I discern objects perspectivally through dynamic modes of selectivity (and enable them to be for me). ('My') consciousness is bound when reflexively I am aware of being aware of a certain content. ('My') consciousness is bound whenever it is in virtue of an intersubjective community of awareness and is dependent upon an other. ('My') consciousness is bound when, as an organic temporality, it is informed by an irrevocable history. ('My') consciousness is utterly bound when its desire-laden contents are completely involuntary. . . .
>
> Consciousness is boundless when, as a power of being, as an essential feature of the self, it is without determinate content. Consciousness is boundless when, unselfconsciously, 'I' am at one with reality.[1]

This analysis of consciousness into two modalities reflects the inherent difficulty of expressing the paradoxical nature of consciousness. Further clarity can be achieved when one recognizes that there is only Being-Consciousness and that the so-called empirical "I"-consciousness is an illusion superimposed on that Transcendental Consciousness. Consciousness, in other

---

1. Eliot Deutsch, *Personhood, Creativity and Freedom* (Honolulu: University of Hawaii Press, 1982), pp. 35-36.

words, is *always* boundless, but because of the play of attention in the manifest domain of existence, there arises the illusion of being bound. Thus, strictly speaking, there is only one primary mode of consciousness, namely Being-Consciousness. What appears as the finite consciousness, in which subject and object are separated, is a phantom that in no way modifies or negates the Transcendental Consciousness.

This is the testimony of the Adepts, who have Realized this uniform Being-Consciousness that is undifferentiated and free of the mechanicalness of Nature. And this perspective is truly liberating, since it grants human beings the innate capacity for total self-transcendence: One does not need to be implicated in the drama of the personal or egoic consciousness. Indeed, there is a movement in reality itself by virtue of which some individuals—possibly in increasing numbers as humanity evolves spiritually—feel "meta-motivated" to Realize the Consciousness prior to the play of selective attention in the finite realms of body and mind. Such individuals are drawn to spiritual (or genuinely self-transcending) life and the discipline and commitment this requires. So long as the material world, and its cause-and-effect laws, are thought to express the fullness of existence, there is no hope for mankind to grow beyond its present level of acute self-obsession. However, once it is understood that the universe is not what it seems to be, but a *psycho-physical* process of immense magnitude and complexity, spontaneously occurring against the backdrop of the Unity of the Being-Consciousness, it is possible to look upon one's individual life, and mankind's generic potential, in a radically different way.

Then life is seen as a school in which spiritual lessons are to be learned. And the Adepts are recognized to be the "specialists" or "experts" who can facilitate this process of learning and readaptation by their Teachings, and more so by their sheer Presence.[2]

But to come to this point of insight and recognition, a person must be willing to drop a good many prejudices and preconceived notions about the world and himself. More likely than not, the majority of people will not be able to inspect and suspend their private cosmology long enough to allow the Adepts' argument to make its point. They would have to struggle against the tide of deeply entrenched beliefs, neurotic expectations, and consoling hopes, as well as the terror of true self-knowledge.

2. Capitalization of terms like "Adept," "Teaching," and "Presence" is a simple device to indicate that these words have a transcendental import. For instance, the Adept's Teaching is Empowered communication, not mere verbal instruction or philosophy. It carries a numinous "charge" that aids others in their ordeal of self-transformation. Because, as will be explained, the Adept is coessential with the ultimate Being-Consciousness, his entire life—every word or gesture—is a direct and spontaneous expression of that Reality. Hence the Adept's behavior is always a confrontation that has the unpremeditated purpose of Awakening others.

Yet, those who are seriously considering or attempting to engage spiritual life must sooner or later confront the extraordinary mechanism that the Enlightened Adept represents. The possibility of maturing and fulfilling one's spiritual practice without a Realized Teacher is exceedingly slight. Many spiritual aspirants in the West, who have been brought up to value independence of mind, subscribe to the view that the best guru is one's own light or conscience, or the Divine Reality directly. They are loath to consider the idea of mediatorship, as they see it, in spiritual matters. And their bias is fueled by the numerous "gurus" who peddle their wares in the spiritual marketplace, but who have little or nothing of real spiritual worth to offer. They are, therefore, rightly concerned about losing their independent judgment in submission to such wolves in sheep's clothing.

At the same time, however, they must realize that the principle of spiritual life is in fact surrender of everything that one seems to be. The need for rebellious independence from any authority is as immature as the need for childish dependence on a teacher. For surrender to be authentic, it must be a mature gesture. That is to say, a practitioner must have clearly understood what is required in his own case to penetrate the armor of the ego and to orient his whole being to the Transcendental Reality, and then simply do whatever is necessary and appropriate.

Surrender to an Enlightened Teacher is not surrender to another ego that may superimpose its will on oneself. In the Adept's case, there is no ego to refract the Light of the Transcendental Being. Therefore, there can also be no personality clash between the Adept and the disciple or devotee. Whatever conflict may arise, it is always in the reluctant devotee. For, the Adept simply reflects back the devotee's own negativity, hesitancy, doubt, and all the other numerous forms of egoic contraction. Simultaneously, the Adept magnifies in the devotee the impulse to Enlightenment and strengthens in him the intuition of the Ultimate Being-Consciousness.

Surrender to the Adept is yielding to the spiritual process itself. It does not, as is popularly feared, turn the devotee into a mindless zombie. The Adept is not motivated to exploit those who come to him for Liberation. Rather, his entire Compassionate Activity is geared to help devotees break loose from their present enslavement to the mindless automaticities of un-Enlightened life.

This booklet offers a rich compilation of excerpts from the talks and essays of a living Adept, Master Da Free John, in which this great God-Realizer addresses the reader directly about the nature, function, and Teaching style of the Adepts, and not least about his own Mission and Work.

The Editors

Note to the Reader

For easy identification all editorial comments are printed *in italics*.

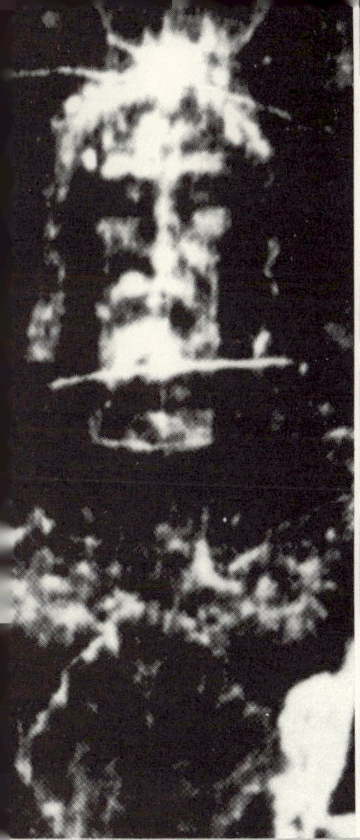

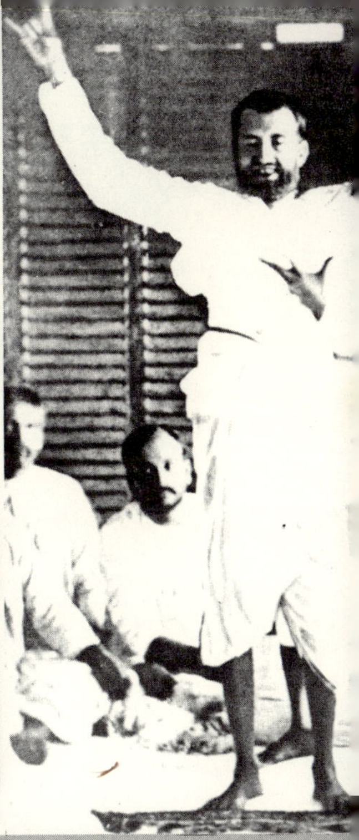

PART ONE

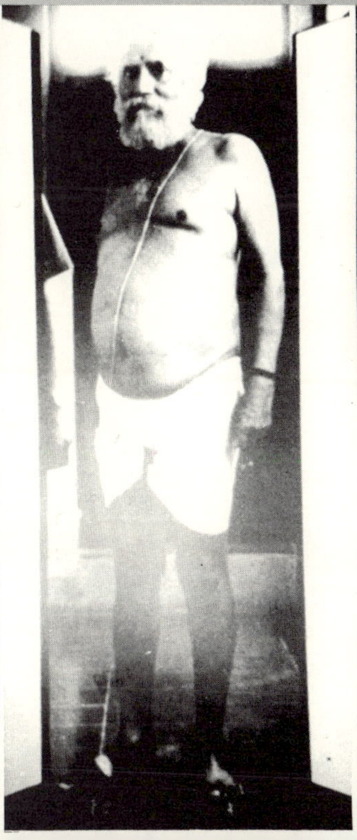

Preceding two pages top row left to right: Swami Ramdas (1884–1963); Sri Ramana Maharshi (1879–1950); Narayan Maharaj (1885–1945); Jesus of Nazareth (d. 33 A.D.), shroud of Turin image; Gautama the Buddha (?563–483 B.C.); Sri Ramakrishna (1836–1886). Bottom row left to right: Brahmajna Ma (1880–1934); Swami Nityananda (?–1961); Shirdi Sai Baba (?–1918); Anandamayi Ma (1896–1982); Sri Rang Avadhoot (1898–1968); Marpa (1012–1097).

The Nature and Work of the Adept

I
Guru Is a Function

Ordinary human life unfolds as a result of the presumed separation from Reality, Being-Consciousness, or God. Yet, even while countless beings live out this illusion of independent existence, the One Being remains perfectly unaffected by the ego's bid for self-rule. More than that, there is a principle active in the manifest realm which works against the egoic illusion of separateness. That principle is the Transforming Power of the Enlightened Adept, who, motivated by a Love-Compassion that is neither egocentric nor altruistic but transcendental, is wholly surrendered to the process of Enlightening others.

Such a being is not a mere mentor, guide, or promulgator of wisdom. Rather, the Adept is literally a Divine Intervention, a mechanism that temporarily interrupts the meandering of conventional life. In Hinduism, beings of this order are known as Avatars. The word stems from the Sanskrit language ("avatara") and means literally "descent." It refers to the unique spiritual process of Divine Incarnation: Having no personal destiny to fulfill, the sole purpose of the embodiment of the Avatar is to confront mankind with the Truth of existence. He demonstrates to humanity the possibility of its own perfection.

The Urgency of the Adept's Work

Mankind needs regular reminders of the fact that it is not fulfilling its highest potential, which is God-Realization. The aspirations and lives of *most people fall far short of this supreme ideal and ultimate necessity. Particularly today, in a time of crisis where the traditions have been eroded by scientism and where the moral fiber of the globe's nations has been undermined, materialistic values reign supreme. In traditional Hindu terms, our period can be characterized as a Dark Age (Kali Yuga) that is in urgent need of the Light and Wisdom of the God-Realizers.*

If you want to learn about Truth when Truth has become corrupted, then go to an Adept. Go to one who has Realized the Truth. Go to one who has already fulfilled the process completely. If you live in a moment in time when there is no Enlightened Tradition, when all the cults are corrupt, you can be certain that somewhere on Earth an Adept is alive. Such a person appears under exactly those conditions, when Truth is no longer visible in the cults, and when religions have become so corrupted by history and fetishism that they are about to become extinct.

The religious traditions in our time are about to be smothered by a mechanistic, political, and scientific world view, only because the cults are in doubt. They have held on to their fetishes so tenaciously that they have lost their association with the Living God. They do not even know the Living God anymore. People who belong to churches, religions, and spiritual societies have no unqualified connection with the Living Reality. There is no true devotion in them, and, therefore, no Realization. Their association with God is only words and hopefulness. Therefore, they do not represent a living force in the world. They have nothing to offer that is Alive. Only the Adepts, who are God-Realized, through whom the Living Power of God manifests, can make a difference in human time. Such individuals are the instruments for the acculturation of humanity. Periodically, such individuals must appear, and they must be influential. There is a notion that Adepts should be hiding in caves in the wilderness. This is not true. If the Adepts do not speak, the only voice that will be heard is that of ordinary people who are not God-Realized. The Adepts are the Sources of spiritual life. Such individuals must therefore enter into the stream of society, to purify the culture and reestablish the process of God-Realization. If they do not speak and become influential, there is no hope at all for humanity.

The Enlightenment of the Whole Body, pp. 155-56

The *Bhagavad Gita* says that "whenever the paths of life are corrupt, and whenever the Law of Association with God has been forgotten, I come." The Divine Consciousness appears in the form of the Spiritual Master who accomplishes the righteous realignment of the Earth and all humanity with God.

The Divine is always doing this kind of work in all the moments of history. The Revelation of God to Man is a process that goes on and on and on. Ultimately, you see, its function is to realign the entire world of Man to God, but the process will not come to an end just because some sort of sacred order has been established on Earth. Everything that exists in all the universes is being brought into alignment with God. The transforming process is a struggle, and until it is ultimately accomplished, the experience of beings is chaotic. Men and women may come to the point of yearning for the Divine Principle, but until the Divine Principle is fully established everywhere, we will not see an order of life based on the salvation of all beings.

The Bodily Location of Happiness, pp. 82–83

The daily world, when viewed from a free position, looks like a great wilderness of tiny acres, each the camp of a single person, who surrounds his small pond with a hedge of immunities, and remains bent upon the water, observing all things reflected there, but seeing nothing directly. The unliberated human world is the wilderness of Narcissus,[1] where he is multiplied as many times as there are human individuals, just as Krishna was multiplied to provide a separate lover for each of his many wives.

The Spiritual Master is indeed a voice that rises in this wilderness, to Awaken every neighbor from the illusion of his acre of land, his ordinary pond, his body-mind. It is a necessary voice, the voice that sounds whenever the Truth of human experience is Revealed to one who is Awake. Therefore, such a one speaks, even with urgency and anger. It is the prophetic voice, the awful shout, expressed with all the gestures of frustrated Divinity.

The Enlightenment of the Whole Body, p. 152

The Adept Is the Source of Religious Life

Religion is founded on the recognition that human life is not limited to the experiential possibilities in the material realm. It is concerned with Man's relationship to the spiritual dimension, however that dimension may be conceived. To the extent that religion preserves this basic orientation, it is authentic and radical. And to the degree that it endeavors to organize Man's social relations in light of a higher moral understanding, it is conventional.

---

1. Narcissus, the self-lover of Greek mythology, is a key symbol in Master Da Free John's description of Man as a self-possessed seeker, one who suffers in dilemma, contracted upon himself at every level of the being from all relations and from the condition of relationship itself.

At the center of authentic religion is always the Creative Impulse of a God-Realized being. Since there is only One Being-Consciousness, the great Adepts are, in their essential Nature, fully identical. However, their Teachings are diverse, and at times even in seeming contrast, because they address themselves to a particular culture and period. But there is no disagreement about the ultimate purpose of their Work—which is to draw others into the same Enlightened Condition—and the nature of their spiritual Transmission.

The primary force and root of all the religious traditions are the Adepts, those who actually Realize the Transcendental Divine Reality. Adepts arise in all times and places and become associated with the movements and complex structures existing in the immediate environment. Throughout their lifetime, both before and after their Realization, they move into the existing culture and associate with its influences. Thus, while their Teaching is an expression of actual Realization, their words reflect and comment upon all kinds of cultural complexities and ideals. Where Adepts or the Realizers of Truth arise, they transform the existing culture, eliminating some aspects of traditional religious and spiritual life and emphasizing others. They are a motion in the midst of the stream of conventions.

The tradition of Truth, of Transcendental Realization, is the tradition of the Adepts. Apart from the Adepts, there is no tradition of Truth.

Don't You Think If You Were Really Being Religious You Would Be Seeing Things by Now? vol. 2, no. 2 (1981), p. 3

In all traditions, a great deal is always made of some key individual. There is no great spiritual tradition that is without a person at the center of the process. How that person is interpreted through the intellectual lore of each tradition varies, but such a person always exists. In other words, the Truth is not separable from a human function, a special human function that is perceived in the form of the Guru. And the Guru is not separable from God. He is not separate from your very Self. The process of spiritual life, then, includes these three principles: the very Self or Real Condition, the Guru, and the Divine. All three are the fruits of spiritual life. All three are its fullness, its enjoyments. The guru seen apart from one's Self, apart from understanding, is not the true Guru. The guru seen apart from God is not the true Guru. God seen apart from the very Self is not the true God. The self, inner knowledge, understanding seen apart from the Guru and God is not true Self-Knowledge. The Guru is the function that arises in the world and serves the illumination of men wherein they know their own Nature perfectly. The Guru is the center of spiritual practice, the center of spiritual life. The relationship to the Guru, Satsang, is the condition of spiritual life, the true principle.

The Dawn Horse, vol. 2, no. 3 (1975), p. 8

The Siddhas,[2] who live in the Form of Truth, are all the same. There is no difference between them. If you place two sticks into one flame, when you draw them out you will have two flames. But they are the same light. Just so, the Siddhas are fundamentally one. But they are functionally unique, just as all manifest entities are fundamentally the generations of one Nature, one Reality, but they are functionally unique.

The Method of the Siddhas, p. 324

The mystical and evolutionary processes of human development have been practiced and transmitted by various kinds or degrees of Adepts throughout human history. Certain founders of religion (such as Jesus and Gautama) were practicing Adepts of this kind. Other religious founders or leaders, such as Mohammed and Martin Luther, were not practicing Adepts, but they were inspired men of insight or prophetic urgency, whose personal activity was entirely within the domain of exoteric religion. But most practitioners or Adepts of the mystical and evolutionary science were active outside the realm of "Everyman," and they were known only within the esoteric "inner circles" of the religious and spiritual traditions.

Lesser Adepts are individuals who have enjoyed remarkable mystical experiences and attained a degree of Wisdom that is helpful or useful to individuals who are less developed than themselves. These lesser Adepts serve the awakening of idealism and functional discipline in ordinary people, and the level of experience to which they lead their followers is generally limited to mystical developments of the Life-Current in the autonomic nervous system and the central nervous system.

However, the highest Adepts serve the awakening of radical insight and responsibility in others, and they guide others through and beyond personal and subjective mysticism, into the domain of the evolutionary transformation

---

2. A Siddha is literally a "Fulfilled" or "Perfect One." A Siddha (also Maha-Siddha, "Maha" meaning great) is one who has Realized God permanently and beyond doubt. Master Da Free John uses the term to refer to the Free Adepts who have appeared in many cultures and who, because of their own Awakening, are naturally moved to Awaken others through the spontaneously transmitted Consciousness, Presence, Power, and Intelligence of the Divine Being.

and ultimate self-transcendence of Man. Therefore, the Work of the highest Adepts is fundamental to human culture as a whole.
Scientific Proof of the Existence of God Will Soon Be Announced by the White House! pp. 355-56

The Superphysics of Spiritual Evolution

From the vantage point of the Enlightened being, life is a school in which the lesson of conscious cooperation with the spiritual Law of ego-transcendence must be learned. The sheer reactivity that marks ordinary human life does not represent mankind's highest evolutionary potential. Rather, humanity's true potential and destiny is realized in the Adept, whose perfect God-Consciousness is the ever-present possibility of Man.

The higher evolutionary process has traditionally been served by individual understanding of the instructions of an Adept, and by individual acceptance of the guidance of an Adept during every stage of practice. And the Adept himself, by higher psycho-physical means, stimulates the central nervous system of others (both in itself and as a means of changing the mental and bodily being via the autonomic nervous system). This process is known in the traditions of religion as spiritual transmission. For these reasons, spiritual Adepts tended and still tend to accept disciples or devotees, and also to create a community or culture of such individuals.
Scientific Proof of the Existence of God Will Soon Be Announced by the White House! p. 353

The Spiritual Master, because of his Transformed psycho-physical Condition, is Radiant and Conscious in the Perfect Identity of Self in God. Therefore, he Functions as an Agent of Transformation in the case of devotees who submit to him in love, in the spiritual manner.

The Spiritual Master is one who has fulfilled the Law in his own Transformation, and who has been Served by the Presence, the Attention, the Glance, the Instruction, and the Touch of others, who were Agents of God. Likewise, he also serves devotees by his Presence, Attention, Glance, Instruction, and Touch.

By such means, the Spiritual Master Awakens and Enlivens devotees with the Radiance of the Divine Person. It is a literal and necessary Process. It is not symbolic, appearing only as ritual. By his Contact with devotees, who make themselves available through devotional Communion with him, the

Spiritual Master Serves the Perfect Purpose of God. His Regard Awakens the soul in the heart, repolarizing the subtler mechanisms, consisting of the cerebro-spinal fluid, the nervous system, the brain, the endocrine glands, and so forth. In this manner, the Power of the heart matures the devotee. The soul is established in Communion with the Divine Radiance by the Touch of the Master-Presence, which purifies and transforms the body-mind, and leads the soul into its Perfect Awakening as the Self at Infinity.

The Enlightenment of the Whole Body, p. 255

The human Spiritual Master is an agent to the advantage of those in like form. When one enters into right relationship with the Spiritual Master, changes happen in the literal physics of one's existence. It is not just a matter of ideas. I am talking about transformations at the level of energy, at the level of the higher light of physics, at the level of mind beyond the physical limitations that people now presume, at the level of the absolute Speed of ultimate Light. The transforming process is enacted in devotees, duplicated in them in and through that Living Company. It is not a matter of conceptual symbolisms or emotional attachment to some extraordinary person. It is real physics. And it is to the advantage of people when someone among them has gone through the whole cycle of Transformation, because they can then make use of the Offering of that Process, that Company.

Most people are willing to sacrifice things, but not themselves. They are willing to pay cash, in other words, for a quick salvation. This is an ancient ritual of worship, but it is false and futile. True worship is the sacrifice of your own bodily being in Truth, in the living and Transforming Company of the Spiritual Master. People absolutely resist that sacrifice. The reason they resist it is that they know nothing about it. They are subhuman in their present level of adaptation. Sacrifice represents another stage of evolution for them. They are incapable of it in their actual, literal, psycho-physical condition. They must be drawn out of that condition, led out into another state of existence. And it is as far to go from where they are now to the ultimate Divine Realization as it is for the amoeba in the primal mud of the Earth to become a human being. Everything about them, even the body, must change radically.

But the changes that must occur are literal, psycho-physical changes, just as literal as if you were to acquire more legs and arms, except that the most dramatic changes occur in dimensions different from the outward shape of the body. Certainly changes occur in the flesh and the elemental structures of the body, but the changes do not really alter its outward shape. The change is as literal as evolving from a dinosaur to a human being, and it is as dramatic as that, but it principally occurs at more subtle levels of the physics of the bodily being. There are literal changes in the nervous system, literal changes in the chemistry of the body, literal changes in the structural functioning of the brain.

You cannot realize such a change in a weekend. Such a change is a living process, a matter of growth. But it can be quickened and intensified through right practice, through real moral or sacrificial discipline, through the Company of the Spiritual Master. In that Company, the Condition of the higher physics is Communicated to the individual, in such a way that it brings about a radical Transformation in the disposition of the body-mind, and then magnifies the effectiveness of that disposition many times, so that the whole process can take place even in a single lifetime. That process can at least be dramatically advanced in one lifetime, if not completely fulfilled.

If you move into such a relationship, the Process begins to duplicate itself in your case. It is not as if you are a robot that is being transformed through the effect of some computer—no, it is a living and human relationship. But it is not like the conventional doctor-patient or mommy-daddy-baby games. Irresponsible people cannot enter into it. You must be responsible for yourself at the human level, and in a profoundly uncommon way. You must live the ordinary discipline yourself. You yourself must be love under all ordinary, daily conditions. You must make a moral change in your life. There is no way whereby you can be relieved of this necessity, and nobody can do it for you. But all of that ordinary personal and moral responsibility simply prepares you for the right relationship to the Spiritual Agency made available by the Divine through the Spiritual Master. Such a one is your unique advantage, because he is present in the same bodily form as you—manifest in this same physical condition, with the same nervous system, the same kind of brain. But in him all of these things are raised to an absolute level of functioning, so that entering into contact or Communion with that individual brings changes even at the level of the psycho-physical body which you bring into relationship with him.

The abstract Deity cannot serve you in that way, you see, because the physics of this Process must be directly present, and the human Demonstration of the Process must be present, in a form that can do its Work in your case. That Work is the purpose of the Spiritual Master, because he represents a state of the ultimate physics of things that is your potential but not your actuality at the present time. The abstract Divine and the potential powers of the universe are just as true as the Spiritual Master, but they are not organized (except in the case of the Spiritual Master) for the sake of the immediate transformation of human beings.

Scientific Proof of the Existence of God Will Soon Be Announced by the White House! pp. 364–68

The Spiritual Master appears, to communicate the Way of the transcendence of self and the transcendence of the present stage of Man—so that mankind may more generally fulfill the higher trend of evolution, rather than fall back upon itself in regressive self-possession and exploitation of the elemental Man. However, the Spiritual Master is also full of Transcendental urgency. He also communicates to Man. He reminds Man that even Man is a moment, a process, grotesque when seen in himself. He reminds Man that his beauty and happiness are in his Ecstasy, his sacrifice toward what is yet to come and what is Perfect. He reminds Man that his true Destiny is not in his own evolutionary fulfillment, but in the fulfillment of the sacrifice of the whole World, which includes everything before and after Man, as well as Man himself.

Scientific Proof of the Existence of God Will Soon Be Announced by the White House! p. 351

The Guru Is a Sacrifice

"Guru" is a Sanskrit term meaning "he who is heavy, weighty." According to esoteric explanation, the two syllables of the word denote "dispeller of darkness." Commonly applied to any spiritual teacher, who may or may not be Enlightened, the word "guru" refers here specifically to the "sad-guru" or True Teacher, whose whole being is "heavy" or pregnant with Truth. He is homogeneous with Reality or Being-Consciousness, and as such he lives as a perfect demonstration of the Law of constant self-transcending sacrifice or surrender.

Guru is not a kind of status. It is a specific function. There are some who awaken, but who simply live, without becoming active as the function of Guru. There are others who awaken and do in fact perform that function. Truth, not the "role" of Guru, is the enjoyment of <u>all</u> who are awake.

The Method of the Siddhas, pp. 36-37

The ordinary devotee does not Awaken at birth with Divine Consciousness. Only God, the Divine Conscious Being, Awakens with that Consciousness in the plane of human beings. The devotee Awakens to the Divine at last through surrender, yes—this is the Great Secret of the Way of Truth, the Way that I Teach. But the Divine

Consciousness or Spiritual Master is a specific function among human beings. A handful of people in all the aeons of human time have been the Purusha,[3] the Consciousness "I am God." Only a fraction of the billions and billions of births of beings that have occurred on the Earth alone have been the birth of the Divine Consciousness. Only the Spiritual Master is that birth.

It is the unique function of the Purusha to save the souls, the "jivas," the un-Enlightened beings. Yet, through ecstasy, through mindless surrender to God, un-Enlightened beings may also Realize God, even as the Spiritual Master has done. The Divine Consciousness is Realizable ultimately by all beings. In the play of existence, however, the Spiritual Master is a different kind of being, a fact that the Spiritual Master must eventually realize!

You must understand that the unique status of the Spiritual Master is not given for his own sake. The Spiritual Master is not a human being with a superior egoic consciousness that he or she is God. The ego of such a one is destroyed, transcended in the process of his or her lifetime. The situation of the Spiritual Master is not as you might imagine. You may be thinking: "We all know you are not suffering like us! We poor bastards are the ones who are suffering—you've got it made!" Well, such thinking is not true at all. The lifetime of the Spiritual Master is only sacrifice, and therefore more a torment than the lifetime of the ordinary soul. Read the biographies of the great Spiritual Masters. They all tell the same story of a life that is terrible in some ways, a life in which frequently they are exploited and rejected, and in which they are under the constant threat of domination by worldly and negative forces. Such individuals are always dealing with great forces, not just mastering their rejection by human beings, but tussling with demonic energy. Such is also the case in my lifetime! What you see in my lifetime is the biography of the Divine Being. This is how the Divine Being must live among human beings.

People who are not truly devotees often feel that they must become like the Spiritual Master, that they must have the status of the Spiritual Master. Such people envy the Spiritual Master, and they will not surrender to him. They only want from him a token, a bit of magic, that will somehow make them like he is. But understand this: No un-Enlightened soul wants to be in the position of the Spiritual Master! If you understood my constant experience, you would not envy it—nor could you endure it! One must be Helped by great Divine Power in order to endure the events associated with such a unique life, in order to pass through such events with a clear understanding of what they are as a Divine Process. Only the Divine has the

---

3. "Purusha" is a classical Hindu term for the Divine Being or the Divine Person, the Conscious Identity of all selves, the "primal Person" or original Self.

power to endure the complete revolution of consciousness. Only the Divine has the power to confront the entire play of manifest existence and master all the forces to which beings are subject. The Spiritual Master engages those forces in actual warfare, whereas devotees in general perceive the same forces to be the play of their natural experience. The devotee does not struggle with the power that produces weather or with the physics of light personified as self-conscious beings, although the devotee is also somehow involved in the same play. The Purusha, the Divine, is the victorious Warrior, the Master of all life.

The Bodily Location of Happiness, pp. 84–85

The Spiritual Master has many functions, to exemplify the Way, to Argue the Way, to Bless devotees, to Interfere with them, to Transmit the Spiritual Influence tangibly to them so that they will then, having understood themselves, be capable of spiritual growth. The function of the Adept does not come to an end. The Adept is the continuous resource and resort of devotees.

The Adept is simply the Agency of That which is to be Realized. He is a useful and remarkable Agency, a unique mechanism in nature, a hole in the universe through which the Transcendental Influence moves to the world. Therefore, this remarkable Agency, when it occurs, should be used. It should be acknowledged and understood as it is. People should know how to relate to it, how to use it as a unique instrument of the Divine. Adepts appear to serve your Realization. Otherwise, as soon as someone entered into the sphere of Perfect Realization, he or she would be Translated, and that would be the end of it. Even if some Great Teaching appeared, there would never be the unique instrument of the Adept.

The Fire Gospel, p. 165

The living Spiritual Master is the ultimate Healer, and the mere Presence of such a one is the most benign healing Influence. Without obstruction or limitation of any kind, the Spiritual Master incarnates the All-Pervading Radiance and Transcendental Consciousness of God. Those who enter his Company enter the very Presence of God. He does not have to perform any special intentional action to heal—though he may in fact exercise specific healing capacities of both ordinary and extraordinary kinds. But his Radiant Presence itself spontaneously purifies, harmonizes, and rejuvenates his devotees whole bodily. It restores them to the Ecstasy of Love-Communion with God and, ultimately, to perfect Realization of God. The

Presence of the Spiritual Master does not merely heal devotees of illness, quirks of character, and subhuman or degenerative habits. It heals us of the entire accumulation of our evolutionary history of embodiment in the world, and it draws us into Divine Bliss beyond the consolations of any form of future embodiment, high and low. This is the greatest and most Sacred Mystery, and it is for this reason that men and women have been advised since ancient times that the most auspicious occupation of Man is living devotion to a Spiritual Master.

The Eating Gorilla Comes in Peace, p. 461

The Spiritual Master serves others through Demonstration, conversation, and Teaching consideration. But all such services are secondary to his mere Presence. He generates many kinds of service culturally, institutionally, personally. But those who make use of all those forms of the Service of the Spiritual Master ultimately become associated with his highest form of Service, which is the Service that occurs in his mere Presence. It is such Service that devotees must come to value, and it is such Service to which they should ultimately find access. It is that Service that they must preserve. The other forms of the Spiritual Master's service are animated one by one, and they may then be left behind in the form of various kinds of Agency. But, as long as he lives, the Spiritual Master is Present as Siddhi,[4] and merely turning to the Spiritual Master through Remembrance is to receive "Darshan."[5]

That same Darshan may be engaged through proximity to certain agents of the Spiritual Master. Turning to the Teaching, going to Sanctuaries, entering into the process of meditation, practicing the disciplines, spending time in the company of particularly mature devotees—all of these practices are not ways of encountering phenomenal conditions in and of themselves but ways of using them as Agency, ways of using them as Association with the Divine, and Alignment to the Source, the Spiritual Master. Another form of Darshan, obviously, is to enter into physical proximity to the Spiritual Master. People should learn how to value and cultivate the mere Presence of the Spiritual Master. They should use the various forms of Agency. They should study, practice, and prepare, and receive that Darshan, either through

---

4. The Sanskrit word "Siddhi" means "power, accomplishment." When capitalized, the term refers to the spontaneous and Perfect Consciousness, Presence, and Power of the very Divine, which is Transmitted through the unobstructed Agency of the Spiritual Master or Siddha.

5. "Darshan" means literally "seeing," or "sight or vision of." This Hindi term commonly implies the spontaneous blessings granted by the Adept or Spiritual Master. The Adept gives his blessings by allowing himself to be seen, meditated upon, or known.

Agency and occasion apart from the physical Company of the Spiritual Master or through occasional access to his physical Company. They should not disturb him in that setting or make secondary demands upon him, but should simply live in that Presence.

Such is the most direct opportunity for Transmission. It is really usable only by people who are prepared, people who can make use of the Siddhi of mere Presence, who are not confined to Agencies. Agencies are of course a major source of this alignment to the Source, but for some people nothing but Agencies, and particularly the most outer forms of Agency, serve. In other words, they could not make any use of sitting in silence in the physical Company of the Spiritual Master, whereas they can make use of studying the Teaching, hearing various kinds of instruction, and making use of other services that help establish the rudimentary discipline in life. They might be able to use the Spiritual Master to give them personal advice or to compensate in many ways for their own limitations or irresponsibility, but such are inappropriate uses of the Spiritual Master. Unless the Spiritual Master at some time in his spontaneous activity is moved so to serve, it is not appropriate to make such demands. Rather, devotees should make it possible for the Spiritual Master to serve simply the ultimate form of Agency.

The Bodily Sacrifice of Attention, pp. 82–83

One who functions as Guru, or Spiritual Master, for his devotees may operate for the sake of those who are not his devotees, but his function in that case is not that of Spiritual Master. In the world, generally, he must serve the crisis of understanding, which confounds the search, all need for consolation, fascination, all need for cultural and cultic games. In the world he may function, if he appears at all, in the role of the prophet, which is essentially an aggravation, a criticism, an undermining of the usual life.

The Guru function is not a public function. It does not appear in public, and it does not invite the public as if the spiritual process were simply something you could decide to do, buy, or believe, and then go ahead and perform. The man of understanding appears in public only in the role of prophet and critic. He does not exploit that search. He turns the questioner back on that quality of suffering, dilemma, and dis-ease that motivates him to take on spiritual practices and other kinds of disciplines or to exploit his life possibilities. The Guru function is essentially hidden until the prior condition of real intelligence, understanding, has been fulfilled. Then the Guru may take the role of Spiritual Master for his devotee.

The Dawn Horse, vol. 2, no. 2 (1975), pp. 34–35

The Paradox of the Divine Person

The idea of the God-Man is alien to materialistic thinking. And in the case of the Adept Jesus, it has provoked a great deal of controversy in conventional theology. How can any being be coessential with the Divine and yet appear to be human? How can it be suprapersonal and personal at the same time? Difficulties in answering these questions only arise when the Divine Reality is presumed to be an Other that exists above or beyond the finite realm of body, mind, self, and world.

However, from the viewpoint of Radical Transcendentalism, as Taught by Master Da Free John and other great Adepts, this problem is merely a pseudoproblem of theology or philosophy. In Truth, there is only the One Being-Consciousness in which body, mind, and world arise as self-modifications. The real "problem" is not the nature of the Adept or Divine Incarnation but the ego that arbitrarily fragments the Whole and presumes discontinuities in the One Reality.

The ego is the process of identifying with a particular modification—the body-mind—of the One Being-Consciousness. In the Adept's case, this limited identification is surrendered in favor of the All-Identity of Being-Consciousness. Thus, the Adept is no longer fooled by the belief in a separate body-mind. Even though "his" body-mind, together with its particular personality, continues to arise within the overall world-process, it has ceased to be his reference point. Or rather, the Adept knows his body-mind to be the total Field of Existence.

This is a great Paradox and a great Truth, which is demonstrated again and again to those who come into the spiritual Company of the Adept and catch a glimpse of his spontaneous Work.

The Appearance of the Spiritual Master in this world is the sacrificial embodiment of the Divine Consciousness, or the "Purusha," as it is named in the Hindu tradition. Such a life is Divine, but it is also paradoxically associated with all the limitations of human existence.

This is how the Purusha breaks through space-time and into human time, by taking up precisely the limitations, even the unconsciousness and the un-Enlightenment, of the human individual. Yet the force of the Realization of the Divine is so profound that the ordinary destiny of the human individual or incarnation is constantly undermined and his or her limitations transcended to the point that suddenly the same human being, with full consciousness, Realizes that he is the Purusha. Such a Realization is given occasionally in human time.

The Divine Being in the form of the Spiritual Master is Transfigured during this lifetime and Awakens to his or her Divine function. Likewise, every individual, every devotee, Awakens, through right relationship to that One, to the ultimate destiny and to the God-Realizing process of existence. God does the work of the Spiritual Master, God creates the lifetime of the Spiritual Master, and God is Awakening as the Spiritual Master. The birth of the Spiritual Master is extraordinary! The Divine Conscious Being appears in the world with the same limitations with which all other beings are born, yet such an individual is more and more profoundly Awakened with full consciousness of the Divine Truth that "I am that One."

The Bodily Location of Happiness, pp. 83-84

The Spiritual Master literally does not exist in the state of the natural human being. The Spiritual Master has Gracefully Realized God, and this Realization is not the same as having one's attention on the Play of God and feeling associated with Divine Influence. God-Realization is literal transcendence of the human condition. The Spiritual Master consciously abides in the Infinite Condition of Consciousness and Energy. Thus, the body of the Spiritual Master is literally, directly, felt by him to be Infinite Energy and Infinite Consciousness. No effort is required in order to feel this Radiant Consciousness. The Energy, the Consciousness of God simply has no obstruction in this body-mind. Attention is not in exile, unillumined, elsewhere. He seems to engage all the ordinary play of attention, but there is no limitation in the heart. There is continuous immersion in the Infinite Force of the Heart,[6] and that Force is Radiant as the body-mind of the Spiritual Master. It also outshines this body-mind, since it is not limited by what the Spiritual Master appears to be.

Vision Mound, vol. 2, no. 10 (1979), p. 15

The longer you live with the Guru, the more your relationship to the Guru becomes itself an intuitive realization of the Divine, because the Guru is not simply a human individual, a cultic figure. The Guru is a specific function in God. The Guru is not exclusively that human person who manifests and demonstrates that function. The Guru's command to meditate on him is not the command to meditate on the human figure, the cultic Guru. It is the command to meditate upon the Divine Person. In fact the form of the Guru is the Divine Form. It is upon the Divine Form, the form of the

---

6. The "Heart" is another name for the Divine Self, the intuition or Realization of the Radiant Transcendental Being or God.

Divine Person, that the Guru invites you to meditate, through the agency of the human relationship between the Guru and the devotee.

Garbage and the Goddess, p. 175

To meditate on the Spiritual Master is to surrender, to participate in Divine Life from the heart. It is to Commune with the Spiritual Master so that, through love, one enters into sympathy with what the Spiritual Master is altogether, not merely that person sitting there with the characteristics you can discover by observation through the senses. The Energy, the Radiant Force of the Master, must be encountered in its Truth as the Heart, as that very Consciousness, prior to all the effects that it may create in the body-mind of the one who encounters it.

Vision Mound, vol. 2, no. 10 (1979), pp. 15–16

You become what you meditate on. Thus, if your feeling-attention is made a sacrifice, so that it becomes <u>absolute</u> feeling-attention, love, or sacrifice to the Spiritual Master, then there is a perfect link between you and the Absolute or Divine Condition. By this means you are lifted out of all the conditional states of life and birth in any form. Therefore, spiritual allegiance to the Spiritual Master is the highest function of existence. It is the single advantage not only of human beings but of all beings. It is a unique function in nature.

If we are mediocre in our attention to the Spiritual Master, if our relationship to him, or her, is conventional or casually indulged while we continue to be driven by tendency, then the function of the Spiritual Master is forgotten. It is denied. It is not effective as described. Only the ego will deny the Spiritual Master or the Divine. The ego wants to do it himself. Do <u>what</u> himself? <u>Be</u> himself. Be untouched. Since you become what you meditate on, you should meditate on, or give feeling-attention to, the Absolute, which, in the form that it is given to you, the Form of the Spiritual Master, is your highest advantage.

The Way That I Teach, pp. 251–52

II
The Right Approach to the Adept

For the person steeped in a materialistic view of the world or even a conventional religious understanding of existence, the Adept is a sheer impossibility or a naive myth that has to be reinterpreted to make any sense at all. But shortsighted denial or "demythologization" of the Adept does not at all curtail his spiritual Function and Influence. This becomes evident to those who enter the orbit of his Presence and find themselves transformed by it.

The Adept is an offense to the worldly ego, the haughty intellect that deems itself to have all the answers. He is an intruder into the life of Narcissus, the "usual man," who contemplates his own image in the pool of his habits and addictions. To see the Adept, a person must look up from the pool and make an altogether different gesture. That gesture goes beyond mere childish dependence, worship, and awe, just as it goes beyond rebellious refutation or querulous defiance.

The Adept Is Not a Cultic Idol

The spiritual relationship between Adept or Guru and devotee or disciple has been vastly misunderstood by the popular mind. Fawning servitude and mindless adulation have no place in this sacred relationship of mutual self-transcendence or love-surrender. The popular caricature is largely derived from the failure of immature devotees to relate to the Adept not as a parent figure or God-substitute but as a transparent symbol of the Divine Reality and as a living Agent of spiritual Transformation.

Spiritual surrender to the Adept does not relieve a devotee of personal responsibility and application, nor does it deprive him of his "personality" as often feared. Rather, what the relationship to the Adept undermines is the devotee's exclusive identification with the body-mind and its changing conditions. Instead of living as a fearful ego, deeming itself locked into a bodily casing and associated with private thoughts, feelings, and sensations, he gradually Awakens to the Fact that there is only the One Identity that is Being-Consciousness, in which his own body-mind and all other phenomena appear and disappear.

The Spiritual Master is not a Surrogate God or a Substitute Sacrifice, but a God-Pointer, a Proof of God and the Way, a Demonstration, a Sign, an Agent of Transmission, and an Awakener of those who are willing to surrender their self-possession. The Way Itself is to live in Freedom, not to be bound by self, any other, or Nature as a whole. Therefore, the relationship to the Spiritual Master is the Context and the Means of Free Realization, and not a justification for popular egoity, childish dependency, adolescent reactivity, conventional social behavior and fulfillment, or any other goal or tendency of the deluded ego.

The Hymn of the Master, pp. 12–13

No thought or figure or any perception arising in the mind is, in itself, God. No thing, no body, no moment or place, in itself, is God. Rather, every moment, place, thing, body, or state of mind inheres in God. Whatever arises should be recognized in God, not idolized as God. Then all conditions become Reminders that draw us into the ecstatic presumption of the Mysterious Presence of the Living One.

A Transcendental Adept or true Spiritual Master is a Transparent Reminder of the Living One, a Guide to Ecstatic Remembrance of the One in Whom all conditions arise and change and pass away. Such an Adept is not to be made into the Idol of a Cult, as if God were exclusively contained in the objective person and subjective beliefs of a particular sect. Rather, right relationship to an Adept Spiritual Master takes the form of free ecstatic surrender to the Living Divine based on recognition of the Living One in the Revelation of Freedom, Happiness, Love, Wisdom, Help, and Radiant Power that Shines in the Company of the Adept. Right relationship to a true Spiritual Master is the most fundamental basis of the universal process that is true religion, and there is no basis for "religious differences" at the level of actual practice and Realization.

Scientific Proof of the Existence of God Will Soon Be Announced by the White House! pp. 314–15

The childish individual depends on the Spiritual Master as on a parent, seeking his loving attention, expecting to be nurtured and consoled and fascinated and saved from death by his Company. He wants to be saved from that for which he must himself be responsible—which is the demand to love and be a sacrifice, even to the degree of death.

The adolescent individual identifies with the Spiritual Master, thinking himself to be identical and equal to the Realization of the Spiritual Master, and thus requiring no Grace, no practice, no transformation. Such an individual likes to engage in casual association with the Teaching and Person of the Spiritual Master, disguising a secret need and intention to become truly the Master's equal (at least in the eyes of others) by mere association. Such a one also likes the glamorized sense of himself that he appears to acquire or about which he boasts, because his casual friendship with the Spiritual Master seems to indicate an acknowledgment of his own superior qualities. He wants to be known for being what he can only Realize in eternal sacrifice into that which includes him but which is not him in his exclusive independence.

The mature individual or true devotee is free of childish and adolescent approaches to the Spiritual Master. He is neither childishly dependent, as upon a parent, nor adolescently independent, as in revolt against a parent. Rather, he turns to the Spiritual Master freely, in love and service, in gestures of surrender to the Process and the Reality that are always Present and Awakening in that Company. Such an individual is not motivated by the neurotic dilemmas and the self-protective searching for solutions that characterize the usual man. He has been awakened to intuition of his own Real Condition and to the native activity of love in service. He has been awakened through "hearing" the argument and "seeing" the Presence of the Spiritual Master. Thus, he is not bound or afraid. He is free to surrender in love to the Agent of his own Destiny, and in such surrender in love he fulfills the Law of practice wherein Grace may be given and transformation made.

The Enlightenment of the Whole Body, pp. 197-98

The cultic guru fascinates and pleases you and lulls you into attachments to himself and his methods. He just keeps you asleep in front of the TV set. He doesn't really serve you. He exploits you, perhaps because he himself has so much doubt about the world and about the Divine. And he himself suffers a poisoned vision of his disciples. He doesn't dare to master his disciple, he doesn't dare create another difficult moment for him. "This poor guy. I know what, I will give him a mantra! Come here, come here. I know it has been heavy, but from now on you just recite 'Harry Umpti-ump,' and the Lord will set it straight for you." But the true Guru doesn't have such an option. He has to get up and arm-wrestle that idiotic disciple. He must curse at him again and be difficult with him, and also continue to maintain himself with humor. Disciples and devotees are as much of a test for the Guru as his own sadhana[1] ever was. If there is anything that can make you

---

1. "Sadhana," a Sanskrit word, is right or true action appropriate to real or spiritual life. The term commonly or traditionally refers to spiritual practices directed toward the goal of spiritual and religious attainment. Master Da Free John uses the term to mean appropriate action generated not as a means to Truth but on the basis of prior understanding.

lose your humor, it is a disciple! But you cannot get into the habit of believing your disciple, whatever his number, whether he plays stupid, or "poor me," or whether he is getting angry, or having a difficult time, or whatever he seems to be doing. None of that is true.

The temptation to create the cult must continually be wiped out. Disciples must not be consoled and fascinated and made unconscious in the cult. They must be quickened. They do not want the crisis of this real intelligence to occur. They want to be served with all those things that will allow them to continue in the drama that they are already creating in order to justify irresponsibility, self-indulgence, and the cycle of concerns that is their peculiar suffering. So the Guru, knowing his disciple only wants to sleep, must continue to shake him and offend him. And he must be offensive with humor, so that he doesn't wind up creating a negative effect on his disciple, but actually serves that transformation, that understanding.

The Dawn Horse, vol. 2, no. 1 (1975), pp. 4-5

John the Beloved always wrote or spoke as an intimate devotee of a Spiritual Master. That is, he was communicating about the Way of true worship, or ecstatic bodily Communion with the Living God, but he always acknowledged his own Spiritual Master (who initiated him into the practice of esoteric Communion with the Living Spirit) as if his Master were identical to the Spirit and thus to God. This is a habit of acknowledgment that is typical of all oriental esoteric societies. It represents a profound acknowledgment and appreciation of the mechanism of initiation, guidance, and ecstatic participation enjoyed in the unique spiritual and esoteric relationship of the devotee and his or her Spiritual Master.

No heresy or delusion is contained in this manner of acknowledgment, unless, as has been the case with the exoteric Christian Church that survived the time of Jesus and John the Beloved, the language becomes exoteric and exclusive. That is, if the language of the ecstatic acknowledgment of a Spiritual Master by his true devotees is inherited by a nominal or exoteric cult, that individual tends to become exclusively identified with the Divine Reality. The result of this is that the Living God ceases to be the principle of experience and practice, but abstracted ideas or beliefs and symbolic personalities become, again, the idolatrous basis of the religion. And the religion, or cult, then ceases to understand itself as one of many possible traditional communities involved in esoteric worship. Instead, the cult tends to see and communicate itself as the only community that possesses the Truth.

Scientific Proof of the Existence of God Will Soon Be Announced by the White House! p. 202

The Adept Is a Demand

Because the Enlightened being is not what he seems to be, that is, he is not a particular body-mind or ego, he constantly frustrates the expectations of those who come into association with him. The ego experiences the Adept's Presence as a direct threat to its survival. This provokes the "usual man" to defend himself against the Adept's Influence by falling into an even deeper contraction. Only the genuine devotee can withstand the Adept's Intensity, because he approaches the Enlightened Teacher in the disposition of self-transcendence. He thus turns what is otherwise only an unsuspected source of aggravation into the "heat" of spiritual practice.

The Guru does not come to satisfy devotees or disciples. A satisfied disciple is still the one he was. The Guru is only interested in the utter, radical dissolution of that whole limitation that appears as his disciple. He is not here to satisfy that limitation, to make it feel comfortable. He is here to return men to their own experience, their always present, chronic experience, their dilemma, their unconsciousness. He is here to return men to that, not to prevent them from seeing it, not to keep them obsessively involved with symbols or yogic stimulations of light or sound, or some complex vision of God, some image of Reality, so they will never experience and recognize their own state. The Guru moves by non-support. He undermines the disciple. He skins him! He does not torture him for fun, but he undermines that process which is his suffering.

The Method of the Siddhas, p. 140

The Guru is a kind of irritation to his friends. You can't sleep with a dog barking in your ear, at least most people can't. There is some sort of noise to which everyone is sensitive, and it will keep them awake. The Guru is a constant wakening sound. He is always annoying people with this demand to stay awake, to wake up. He doesn't seduce them within the dream. He doesn't exploit their seeking. He is always offending their search and their preference for unconsciousness. He shows no interest in all of that. He puts it down. He is always doing something prior to the mind. He always acts to return you from the mind, from fascination.

The Method of the Siddhas, p. 152

Satsang is not here to make you forget that drama of your suffering. The Guru has not come to console you with pleasant and hopeful distractions. He always functions to return you to that state, that activity of avoidance. Satsang does not fulfill your search. Satsang acts, by a subtle frustration of your search, to return you to your dilemma, so that it may be understood. The power of intensification that is alive in Satsang is active in the very seat of dilemma. The Shakti[2] of Satsang operates in the dilemma. The crisis in consciousness is sadhana. The suffering and the intensity is sadhana. Sadhana is not merely the pleasantness, it is not the forgetfulness, not the easiness, not the drifty-blissful, smiling and stupid meditation of a man sitting cross-legged in a dog costume. Sadhana is living intelligence, conscious in dilemma, but with intensity. The sadhana of Satsang with the true Guru makes a difference!

It is not that the disciple should not go through the dilemma of his suffering. He must go through it. It is only that, even though he is going through it, he should continue to maintain himself in the condition of Satsang. The greatest mistake people make is to abandon Satsang when they begin to experience its "tooth." No, even this crisis in relation to Satsang itself must come. It comes in everyone's case, now or later. And it comes in an incredibly powerful and seductive form, usually very soon after one begins to experience the Guru's discipline. And it always involves the feeling that you should abandon Satsang, abandon this mad Guru. The first form of this crisis is always a personal conflict with this work and this place. And if the disciple gets through that one and stays, the next time it comes in the form of self-doubt rather than Guru-doubt: "It's not working for me. This sadhana is not possible in my case. I'm damned. I'm too crazy. I'm not ready for it." But if the disciple gets beyond these two times, from then on, for the most part, he deals with all such phenomena as qualities of his hidden strategy, this avoidance of relationship, the drama of Narcissus.

The Method of the Siddhas, p. 136

Spiritual life is a demand, it is a confrontation, it is a relationship. It is not a method you apply to yourself. Your "self" is this contraction, and this contraction is what must be undermined in spiritual life. Therefore, the Guru comes in human form, in living form, to confront you and take you by the neck. He does not merely send down a grinning photograph, to be

---

2. "Shakti" is a term for the living conscious Force or Divine Cosmic and Manifesting Energy or Spiritual Power, the Life-Current of the Living God. When capitalized, the term refers to the universal or perfect Divine Power. When written in lower case, the term refers to that same Power in the form of various finite energies and activities, high or low, within the individual, as well as the generative power and motion of the cosmos.

reproduced with a few fairy comments for everybody to believe. The traditional images and records of past help serve very little. At best they may help a person move into a position where he can actually begin spiritual life. But Truth must come in a living form, absolutely. Truth must confront a man, live him, and meditate him. It is not your meditation that matters. Truth must meditate you. And that is the Siddhi or marvelous process of Satsang. Even while Truth is meditating you in Satsang, you are busy doing more of the usual to yourself, waking yourself up, putting yourself to sleep, reacting in every possible and unconscious way to the force of Satsang, but you are being meditated.

You cannot be "meditated" by one who is not alive. Even if you believe in one who is no longer alive in human form, you cannot provide the necessary, living means for this meditation. Truth must come in living form, usually in the human vehicle of the Guru, the true man of understanding. Spiritual life involves this marvelous process, this Siddhi, this Satsang. If this Siddhi or living spiritual process is not activated, it doesn't make a damn bit of difference what exotic or humble spiritual methods you apply to yourself, for it will always be of the same nature. It will always amount to a form of this contraction. All of your methods, all mantras, all yogic methods, all beliefs, all paths, all religions are extensions of this contraction. Truth itself must become the process of life, and communicate itself, create conditions in life, and make demands, restoring the conscious participation of the individual. Dead Gurus can't kick ass!

The Method of the Siddhas, pp. 224-25

Merely to be in the Company of the Spiritual Master does not produce Enlightenment, or even pleasurable experience! People who are intimately associated with the person of the Spiritual Master may not be devotees at all. They may, in fact, have a great deal of difficulty, or their life may be very pleasurable but without spiritual consciousness. In the history of the spiritual and religious traditions there are countless stories of individuals who have been close to the Spiritual Master (or to an individual with a spiritual function of one or another kind or degree) who ultimately betrayed that individual or were very unhappy in his (or her) company.

There is only one Law, and its demonstration in any individual's case depends on whether he or she is self-possessed or self-surrendering. Those who are self-possessed will be purified, but the force of the Spiritual Master offends them or manifests as difficulties in their lives. Without any malicious intention on his part, or even any intention at all, the Force of the Spiritual

Master can cause pain, difficulty, suffering, and even illusion in the case of an individual who presumes to enter into and exploit the Company of the Spiritual Master without surrendering, like a thief who has come to steal. Such individuals may have difficulty or seem to be enjoying themselves, but in any case they delude themselves in the midst of enjoyment.

Those who approach the Spiritual Master as devotees are likewise purified, but they are also transformed and ultimately Enlightened. Their history is benign, but not merely pleasurable in the conventional sense. Those who approach the Spiritual Master as devotees, in the mood and action of true surrender, by virtue of that relationship are given the Grace, the Force, the Power of transformation and liberation by the Spiritual Master. Nevertheless, they are responsible for the results of their actions. The Spiritual Master cannot determine the destiny of the individual beyond this choice for which the individual himself is responsible. The Master can work in all kinds of ways to instigate this choice, to awaken the individual to choose to surrender, but until he (or she) realizes surrender, the Law determines his experience. If he is not surrendered, he is deluded. His spiritual life, to whatever degree he may think he is involved in such a life, becomes difficult and offensive to him. Anything pleasurable that he realizes in the Company of the Spiritual Master serves to delude him and make him more self-possessed. Once the individual is awakened by the argument and Presence of the Spiritual Master, however, then the Force of that Company begins to purify and transform him. The Company of the Spiritual Master serves the self-transcendence, the surrender, the sacrifice in God, that the individual's total life must ultimately represent. Therefore, those who surrender to the Spiritual Master are Enlightened.

Vision Mound, vol. 2, no. 11 (1979), pp. 34-35

The Spiritual Master Incarnates the Radiant Transcendental Consciousness as Man. Thus, he manifests not only human qualities but the Divine Qualities.

All experiences, positive or negative, arise within or as modifications of the same Divine Radiance or Transcendental Consciousness. Therefore, those who presume to live in the Company of the Spiritual Master are given experiences, but always according to the Law of God. If they surrender themselves to the Spiritual Master in God, and if they constantly transcend themselves through Love-Communion with the Living God under all conditions and via all psycho-physical functions, then they are given the benign Destiny that purifies and Enlightens. However, if they approach like thieves, merely imitating devotees in order to gain self-glamorizing experiences and worldly status, or if they simply refuse the Spiritual Master, and thus the Divine Person, by their self-possessed and self-meditative ways, then they are given the negative or self-defining destiny that binds the body-mind to its own limits and excludes the Realization of the Radiant Transcendental Consciousness.

This is the Divine Law, and its effects are inevitable.

The Bodily Location of Happiness, p. 71

III
The Radical Relationship

Right relationship to the Adept is right relationship to the spiritual process itself. And what this entails is nothing short of the total transformation of the human being, not in the form of an accelerated self-improvement but as uncompromising self-transcendence. What the Adept offers to all beings is God-Realization, or the Condition of True Relationship (or Satsang). This is a radical relationship because it involves the very Root of one's existence. Strictly speaking, though, it is no relationship at all, because in the Ultimate Condition there is no separation from any other; there is no "me" or "you" which could be related to each other. There is only the One Being-Consciousness in which myriads of phenomena—all the countless "me's" and "you's"—arise.

The Adept's Work is to draw his devotees more and more into this Infinite Circle of Being. He helps them to generate and cultivate, from within the Wisdom of their own being, the disposition of heartfelt relationship to everything, of fearless surrender to the conditions of life. This is only possible because one's real Identity is never out of relationship. Only the paranoid ego experiences itself in opposition to other egos or objects, thereby denying and burying the Happiness that is Man's true nature.

The Relationship to the Adept Transcends the Verbal Teaching

The literate mind tends to fasten on words rather than their meaning—a bias not unknown in earlier times, as may be gathered from the Biblical saying, "The letter killeth, but the spirit giveth life" (2 Corinthians 3:6). Even though language is Man's most sophisticated tool for communicating about the world, it is barely adequate when it comes to conveying subjective states and inner experiences. And it is as good as useless for communicating the nature of Ultimate Existence, as the mystics and great Adepts of all times have consistently pointed out. Yet, the verbal communication of the Adept's Teaching is a significant part of his Work, particularly at a time when great store is placed on intellectual understanding.

However, the Adept's real Work takes place in a different dimension. If he had to rely on language alone, his Mission would be doomed to failure. As it is, his verbal Teaching merely attracts the devotee's attention, leads him into a profound consideration of the Adept's argument, and thus opens him up to the benign Influence of the Enlightened Teacher.

There are many "teachers" in the world. There are men of experience of all kinds. There are men of practical experience, of worldly experience, of mystical experience. There are men of every kind of experience. Human beings, like all manifest beings, arise within the material or conditional universes, the manifest, created cosmos, visible and invisible. They live according to the laws of karma, the laws of tendency, function, and repetition. They tend to live from the point of view of that from which they seem to have come, which is the manifest universe itself. And they acquire experience, hour to hour, life to life. Thus, because of the essential inequalities that necessarily arise whenever experience enters the picture, each man or woman acquires a different amount and kind and complex of experience. Here and there people arise who, because of superior acquisition of certain kinds of experience, teach others. Now they may teach the weaving of lovely cloths, or plumbing, or nuclear physics, or English literature. Or they may teach so-called spiritual things, on the basis of their experience. And among those who are thus experienced in the karmic realms, there are some, a rare few, who are genuine saints, genuine men and women of experience, of practical and subtle wisdom, who have realized many things about their own adventure and their own tendencies.

But there is another process that enters the manifest world from the unmanifest dimension. There is a vast, unlimited dimension of existence, not qualified in any sense, not qualified in the way this dimension is, or in the way the infinite variety of conditional, cosmic worlds are. And there is a movement down out of that dimension, that realm of very Light. Living beings appear within the human world, and in many other worlds as well, who have come directly out of the unmanifest or uncreated Light, the Light of the God-World. These are the great Teachers, the World-Teachers, the Siddhas, the Heaven born ones. Their Teaching is not from the point of view of experience. Their Teaching is from the point of view of Truth, Truth already realized, the unattainable (because it is always present) Reality. Those who teach from the point of view of experience teach the search, because they know on the basis of experience that they can grow, that they can approach a subtler and subtler level of realization. The gospel of those who arise within the condition of the material worlds is always a form of seeking. But the Siddhas, those who come down out of the uncreated Light of God, speak from the point of view of the already realized absolute Truth. They come in the

Intelligence, Power, and Form of Real God. Hence, their Teaching is always radical. They do not teach the motives, ways, and forms of seeking, for these are founded in dilemma, not of Truth. And they apply only appropriate conditions to their students, their disciples, and their devotees. They demand only the conditions that are appropriate to be lived, seeing as how Truth is always already the case. Such a one, found alive among his disciples, is the Truth in the world. And he generates in his company the conditions of the Truth, the conditions of the Light of Real God.

The Method of the Siddhas, pp. 323-24

Those Adepts who have actually completed (and thus gone beyond) the "sadhana" or practice based on either of the two conventional propositions begin at last to express themselves in different terms about the matter of Realization and Reality. They may prefer silence (or nonverbal transmission, as in the case of Ramana Maharshi), or they may engage in the strategy of denial of the applicability of conventional language to the description of That which is Realized (as was the case with Gautama), or they may behave strangely and speak in paradoxes or in the form of apparent nonsense (as in the case of certain individuals in the Ch'an or Zen tradition and in the Crazy Wisdom tradition), or they may try to construct a language of philosophy that is compatible with ultimate Realization (as in the cases of Nagarjuna and Shankara). Even all of these forms of communication and transmission may be used by Awakened Adepts, and my own Teaching Work is an example of the use of all such possible means.

All "Completed" or seventh stage[1] Adepts are faced with the fact that the conventions of language and behavior (even of traditional philosophical language and the prescribed behavior of traditional religious and spiritual practice) are all based on the phenomenal, psycho-physical, and thus necessarily egoic point of view. And what the Adept would and must communicate or transmit is the Transcendental Reality, or Awakened Realization of the Transcendental Condition of all phenomenal conditions.

Nirvanasara, pp. 133-34

Therefore, the Spiritual Master communicates a Teaching that is itself a Paradox. That is, the Teaching, or the communication of the Way of Truth, is of such a nature that it contradicts, or upsets, or undermines the established trend of experience, knowledge, communication,

---

1. Master Da Free John has described the development or spiritual evolution of the human individual in terms of seven stages of eternal life. For a description of this unique model, see the Appendix, pp. 97-103.

or self-existence. Through confrontation with the Argument of the Spiritual Master, and by practice of the Way he establishes, individuals are confounded and disturbed, and their ordinary destiny is interrupted. Such is true "hearing." [2]

But the Spiritual Master does not rely on any form of communication to Awaken others. Rather, he uses his Argument only as a goad and a guide to that disposition of equalized awareness wherein the two-sided body and brain is whole and "on the mark." Those who respond to the Argument are then welcomed into the Company of the Spiritual Master, wherein the Divine Truth is to be Realized directly, prior to any kind of communication, or experience, or self-awareness.

In that Company, all communications are undermined. All experiences come and go in that Company, and nothing remains. The self is interrupted in its games of glory and eternal survival. Ultimately, nothing is said, nothing is experienced or made known. The Spiritual Master abides in the Radiance of Divine Ignorance, prior to the body-mind, prior to Man and the World—prior to all communication. He is more than silent, and more than speech. And only those who are Awake at the center may intuit That which the Spiritual Master always Demonstrates, even while he lives. Such devotees truly "see" and "hear" the Spiritual Master. Such devotees are truly initiated into the absolute "Vision" of God, wherein not self or any object, high or low, stands out from the Radiant Bliss.

The Enlightenment of the Whole Body, pp. 244–45

The verbally communicated Dharma[3] is delivered essentially to beings who apparently have minds, who appear to function with the mental vehicle. So the communicated, verbal Dharma is usable only by human beings. The Dharma in Truth, the Dharma that is Truth, that is the Siddhi, that is the Guru-function, is communicated to all beings in all times under all conditions. And the Guru in Satsang is in fact not identical to the Teaching which he gives to human beings, which stands by itself and which they can confront. The Guru in Satsang serves all beings. He communicates a Satsang in which even the frogs may participate, and in fact many do! All

---

2. "Hearing" and "seeing" are technical terms used by Master Da Free John to describe the conscious and spiritual Awakenings that are the necessary foundation of the Way that he Teaches. "Hearing" is the intuitive understanding of the self-contraction and simultaneous intuitive awakening to Divine Consciousness that arise on the basis of disciplined study of the Argument of the Adept. Hearing leads naturally to "seeing," which is emotional and total bodily awakening into faith, or direct feeling-intuition of the Divine Reality under all circumstances.

3. The Sanskrit term "dharma" literally means "Law," and here stands for the ultimate and necessary Way of Life. The word also refers to the verbal Teaching whereby the Great Adepts communicate the Divine Truth and the Way to humanity.

kinds of creatures, even the walls, participate in that sadhana with the same variations of intensity that appear among human beings who deal with the verbal Teaching.

In this light, one of the most obvious limitations of the traditional dharmas, which communicate the way of Truth by identifying it with various experiences, phenomena, symbols, and visions, is that from their point of view none of that stuff is available to anything less than a human being or really of interest to anything more than a human being. All those mysticisms and other artifacts of yoga and religion really belong, if they belong to anything useful, to the verbal or human communication of the Dharma. Frogs, after all, cannot do kundalini yoga![4] There are many beings who do not have the functional capacity to do yogic sadhana or to enjoy realizations of the mind or superconsciousness, because those realizations depend on the vehicle of the mind. Vital beings less than man do not have the vehicle of the mind by which they may transcend the mind, and therefore they cannot do a superconscious sadhana. They cannot do yogic sadhana in its usual sense.

On the other hand, all beings may realize the Heart, whether they are vital beings or human beings or godlike subtle beings. So the Dharma of the Heart, of radical Understanding, is available to all beings. It is the ultimate Truth and condition of all beings, and it is communicated in fact to all beings. Because the human Guru has the vehicles useful to humanity, he seems to be serving human beings exclusively, but in truth he is serving all beings, and not necessarily even individuated beings. He serves the world manifestation in total, on every level, above the world, within the world, in the lower dimensions of the world. And literally—it is not merely an amusing metaphor—the walls do sadhana. Everything does sadhana. The particles of the air do sadhana. The plants do sadhana. All creatures, inanimate things, material things, as well as human beings and beings beyond the human and within the human, all of these are available to the Guru-Siddhi and the Guru-function.

The Dawn Horse, vol. 1, no. 1 (1975), pp. 4-5

---

4. The kundalini or kundalini shakti is the "serpent power," that manifestation of the Force of Life which lies dormant in Man, traditionally described as coiled at the base of the spine. It may be awakened spontaneously in the devotee, after which it ascends along the spinal axis, producing all the various forms of yogic and mystical experience.

Master Da Free John indicates that the internal spiritual force is eternally Awake, but Man is not Awake. Therefore, he recommends no efforts to awaken this force directly, but puts all attention on the Awakening of the individual to his or her prior, eternal, and always present Condition via the conscious process of radical understanding.

Devotion to the Guru

The devotion that the Adept expects of his devotee is one of mature self-surrender to the Truth or Reality. Although a devotee may, at first, fall short of this requirement, his spiritual growth is intimately connected with his increasing understanding that the Adept is not the body-mind in front of him. Thus, when the Adept admonishes him, "Turn to Me and love Me," this is a call for the devotee to orient his whole being to the Transcendental Person, not the embodied being that is apparently relating to him as Teacher.

The mature devotee knows, however, that the Adept's body-mind is literally devoid of an ego and hence nondistinct from the Absolute Reality itself. Therefore, when he bows to the Teacher's physical frame, he bows to the Great One Who is none other than his own true Identity.

The devotion to the Guru commonly described in Hindu and other spiritual or mystical traditions is, above all, devotion to a source which fulfills the spiritual search, a yogi-initiator or great-soul who grants experiences. But I speak of devotion to the Guru in other terms. I speak of such devotion only in the context of true Satsang, which is prior fulfillment, the condition of Truth. I do not speak of the Guru as one who fulfills the yogic search for experience, but as one who undermines and transcends both seeking and the experiential fulfillment of seeking.

The true Guru is not different from Truth. He is simply the function of God. He is not an idol, a fascination. He does not attach individuals to his conditional presence, but leads men to enjoy the Perfect Presence and Reality in the condition of relationship. His instrument is the relationship and mutual drama of the Guru and his perfect devotee. This relationship or drama is the special, immediately salvatory function and process of God. That same Satsang is available apart from his physical presence and after his death in the form of respectful, intelligent, and loving obedience to his radical or perfect Presence, his Teaching, and his Community. The Satsang he teaches is the Eternal Principle which is the very condition of all beings, and which was always their condition even before the human form of the Guru appeared. While the Guru lives he teaches that Satsang which can be enjoyed by all even after his death, not in the special form it may be enjoyed by a relative few during his lifetime, but which could have been enjoyed by all prior to his lifetime. He acts to help his disciples and devotees to realize this form of Satsang even while he lives in the world. The purpose or function of his life is to make this true Principle of Satsang known, and to guarantee the perpetuation of the Teaching and Practice of Satsang beyond his lifetime.

The Method of the Siddhas, p. 314

DA FREE JOHN: The Guru is not other than oneself.

DEVOTEE: What about the rest of humanity?

DA FREE JOHN: Neither are they. They, along with you, may temporarily be living as if they were other and separate, but the Guru does not. "Others" function as others. Being others, they create circumstances or apparent conditions for you to enjoy, for you to suffer. The Guru is not an "other," nor does he live as an other in any sense. One who sees an individual whom others claim to be functioning as Guru may consider him to be an other, like himself. But he has only failed to recognize that one as Guru. The Guru is one's own nature. Absolutely, not symbolically, the Guru is one's very consciousness. This is the literal truth of one who appears as Guru in human form. He is not an other. Therefore, others have no role whatsoever in the transformation that is Truth. Only one's own Self performs that role.

One's relationship with the Guru, which is Satsang, depends on the subtle recognition of the Guru as Truth, as one's own Nature, the Self. That recognition does not necessarily appear at the level of the mind, as mental certainty, or in the form of some sort of visionary or psychic perception. But there must be a subtle recognition. That genuine recognition has no explanation, no mental force in many cases. But that recognition is what allows the relationship between Guru and disciple to be enjoyed as it is, as Satsang, rather than the usual communication of "others."

The Method of the Siddhas, pp. 302-303

The first obstacle, and the primary obstacle, to spiritual life is the relationship to the Guru. It is also the fundamental condition, content, and source of spiritual or real life. If it were not for that, everybody could become spiritual by the mere practice of some method or another. They would read books, they would manipulate themselves with arbitrary beliefs. But spiritual life is a relationship, a living demand. It creates an obstacle from the very beginning. And that obstacle provokes the crisis and fundamental sacrifice that real life requires.

Nothing is offered but Satsang. Nothing is given but that relationship, because it is Truth. Those who finally live it as the condition of life receive everything, because that relationship is the medium of Truth. Everything rests on a man's ability to realize that relationship.

The Method of the Siddhas, pp. 200-201

All of the great Siddhas, the realized ones, who have taught in the world, have given Satsang to their disciples as grace. That was their essential activity and gift. They did not come to give a method, to give a conceptual teaching only, to create a myth, a structure for the mind, some sort of mentality. They brought <u>themselves</u>. They entered into <u>relationship</u> with the world, with their disciples. That relationship is the very structure and outward sign of the process I have described. <u>That</u> is spiritual life. That process is spiritual life.

The Method of the Siddhas, p. 226

The Guru is not just a human person who can have human effects on you. The Guru is active, present as that Siddhi. The Guru is communicated to you under all conditions, twenty-four hours a day. Once that contact is established, once that relationship is established, that Siddhi communicates itself under all conditions, in all states.

No Remedy, p. 26

There is no end to the numbers of living beings who can do this sadhana. The sadhana of relationship to the Guru is a condition which the disciple must realize and live. Since the Guru always, already enjoys it, it takes up none of the Guru's time. There is no limitation to the Guru's capacity to be that fundamental enjoyment for all beings. The limitations are on the disciple's activity within the life-appearance, and on the Guru's apparent activity, the activity of the man of understanding, within that same appearance. But those limitations are only the forms of pleasure and communication, wherein we represent our understanding to one another. Even so, the Guru is rising above the house. He is not this limited state. He is your own enjoyment, perfectly known.

The Method of the Siddhas, p. 174

You must begin to grasp the nature of Satsang. Realizing the principle of Satsang is the same as coming into the human presence of the Guru. The mind falls apart, and the phenomena of the Spiritual Process arise spontaneously. It is not that you must develop a technique for remembering the Guru in some artificial way, but you must truly be present with the Guru, and the Guru must truly be present to you. All of the remembering of the Guru that you can generate will be useless, until the principle of Satsang itself is established, until you find the Guru always.

It is easy enough to find the Guru when he is standing in front of you, or sitting there talking and engaging in obvious actions that the senses can recognize. Sitting in the presence of the human Guru and contemplating his form, you are actually concentrating on the perfect Nature or Reality that is the Guru, truly. Thus, the human form of the Guru is an instrument of meditation, because you can find the Transcendental Form of the Guru through the obvious human presence and form. The human form of the Guru is a Grace, it is given, it is obvious. You need not do very much to find him, and by openly remaining with him when you are present with the Guru, you contact his perfect Form, and the mind dissolves.

But when you are not in the Guru's physical presence, you must be more adept. You must have understood something, learned something, so that you can find the Guru when he is not physically present. And when you do, you notice again that the mind falls apart, regardless of how much thinking about the Guru you may do. You may identify Satsang by a certain sign, which is that the mind falls apart in the presence of the Guru. So if, when you are not in the Guru's physical presence, you notice that the mind is falling apart, you are in Satsang. If, when you are not in the physical presence of the Guru, you do not experience this dissolution, this Spiritual Process, all the time, you are not in Satsang.

The purpose of the human Guru is not to make it easy for you to find him. The purpose of the human Guru is to establish the principle of Satsang independent of his physical presence, because his physical presence is mortal and temporary. Therefore, the physical form of the Guru must be used for its appropriate purpose, which is to establish true Satsang in the world, not just to make it available to a relative few who contemplate the Guru's physical form, because such contemplation is temporary and brief.

The mere activity of sitting with the Guru generates a quality people find desirable, and they become addicted to that contact. They make an idol out of the human Guru, because they notice that very pleasurable things occur when they are in his physical company. But the Guru is not present to become an idol. He is here to instruct you and to transform the tendencies of life, so that Satsang can be lived all the time by everybody who is the least bit inclined to it, independent of the physical presence of the Guru.

The Guru is always testing his devotee to see if the devotee can find the Guru when the Guru is not physically present. Thus, the devotee may experience brief meetings with the Guru and then separations. When the devotee is able to find him always, then the Guru is satisfied. His function has been fulfilled. The devotee's realization of Satsang in a sense frees the Guru of his own mortality, because the function of his mortal presence has been fulfilled and is no longer necessary when the devotee has begun to live independent of the physical presence of the Guru. Not that all of a sudden the devotee is just not interested, or thinks that the physical, human Guru is an illusion. Rather, he feels the principle alive in the human Guru to be omnipresent, and this realization increases the intensity of his respect for the human Guru.

The Guru prepares people to live that Satsang which they could have enjoyed even before his human appearance. Such is the true form of Satsang, not the cultic or ritualistic enjoyment of the impression he left behind him as a human teacher. Invariably we find that when a Guru appears in the world and begins to Teach, he becomes the center of a group of people, so that after his death his human image survives as the cultic object of his Teaching. There is no Satsang then, but only people continuing with the imagery, and the Teaching of the Guru becomes religion, or enthusiasm without understanding and without the true Spiritual Process. The human Guru is an instrument of Satsang, or the true Principle, and after his death of course it is useful to remember and honor him, but not in a cultic way independent of Satsang.

Crazy Wisdom, vol. 1, no. 4 (1982), pp. 34–35

The Devotee Does Not Choose the Adept

The potential devotee is typically a seeker. In his escape from un-Happiness and search for lasting fulfillment, he goes from teacher to teacher, hoping for a quick remedy or solution to his existential problem. When he finally feels he has found the one who could help him out of his spiritual bankruptcy, he may even congratulate himself on his discernment and apparent success. Yet, as Master Da Free John makes quite clear, it is always the Guru who chooses the devotee, just like a flame attracts all kinds of moths. He once remarked that his own devotees were rendered to him before all time, thus affirming a profound transcendental relationship with every one of his devotees.

This also explains the surprising fact that many people are perfectly able to grasp the Adept's argument and are even sympathetic to it, and yet will not commit themselves to the relationship he offers. Of course, they could do so at any given moment, provided they were willing to fully inspect those tendencies that hold them in a position of fearfulness, doubt, or simply lack of determination. Without such radical inspection they will not confront the basic un-Happiness and bondage of their life.

One must choose to be Free, Happy, or God-Realized. Only then does the Enlightened Teacher have a window into which he can beam his Light.

To move into the presence of the Guru is not something the disciple does. He does not actually go to the Guru. He cannot decide one morning to go to him. He doesn't know where the Guru is. How can he go to the sunlight? The disciple is somebody lying asleep in bed. He doesn't go to the Guru. The Guru is the sun, rising, intensifying the light, until the disciple realizes that he is in that presence. That realization is Satsang. And understanding is itself true waking, true knowledge, or recognition of the "sunlight." All seeking for the Guru, all going after the Guru is an activity within the dream. The Guru cannot truly be found within the dream.

The Method of the Siddhas, pp. 172-73

All that occurs for any man or woman is this process I have been describing. The search winds down. The individual falls somehow into his ordinariness, his simple suffering. Then he becomes available to Satsang. When he begins to live Satsang as his real condition, associated with it may be feelings that he has chosen one Guru among others. But such "choices" are purely secondary. In fact, there is no choice. There is only the sudden availability of one who truly functions as Guru. In the life of every true disciple, there has only been the sudden communication of the Heart.

The Method of the Siddhas, p. 309

It is intuition of Reality itself that leads a man to the Guru, and to maintain himself in his company. All "reasons" for holding on to the Guru fall away, and also all the reasons for not holding on to him. None of these reasons has any ultimate significance. The affinity of your nature, your intuition of your nature, the Heart, is entirely responsible for this sadhana.

The Method of the Siddhas, p. 177

The Guru Enters the Devotee

One cannot place a gift into a clenched fist. So long as a person is oblivious to his self-contraction, there is no space for the Adept to work his Miracle of spiritual transformation. Self-understanding is the key to the conscious cooperation with the spiritual process that is continuously initiated in others by the Enlightened being. The Adept cannot help but impinge on his environment. Master Da Free John once observed that even the walls must engage spiritual practice in his company.

Understanding is fundamental to the emotional conversion that must occur for the seeker to turn into a devotee. The egoic contraction must be seen for what it is—in every moment; only then can it be transcended through the disposition of love-surrender or radiance to infinity.

When the Guru enters the devotee, the devotee does not become possessed by the person of the Guru. Rather, the Transcendental nature of the Adept coalesces with the being of the devotee so that the latter's natural self-possession dwindles and he becomes sensitive to the Being-Consciousness that is his permanent true Condition. This mysterious process is the unique gift that the Adept brings to his devotee.

The Guru assumes your Enlightenment. He does not mechanically enlighten you, or give you something to do to enlighten yourself. He absorbs you. He is you to begin with, but the Guru in human form consciously assumes your Divine state in every function in which you appear. He assumes it in your very cells and literally, actively lives you. The Guru literally meditates you. He is in a position to do so, since he is you. The mystery of that process is how this kind of spiritual life is generated and fulfilled. It is fulfilled from the beginning. That Satsang is perfect. The devotee, a piece at a time, begins to become aware of the perfection the Guru has already generated in his case.

No Remedy, p. 83

The Siddha-Guru contacts his disciple in the Heart and at this place behind the eyes. Once that contact is established, the communication between the Guru and his disciple is continuous. It is not limited to the level of life. It is prior to life. And so it goes on and on, twenty-four hours a day, under all conditions, in all states, even beyond death. The contact is continuous. The communication of force is continuous. That is why disciples continue to have experiences of various kinds, whether awake, asleep, or in dreams. The contact and its communications are continuous. The karmas are continually being shuffled, awakened, run through, intensified, purified, obviated.

There is a profound spiritual principle involved in this relationship between the Guru and his disciple. Once he has contacted the disciple in the Heart, and with his own Light in the ajna chakra,[5] the place behind the eyes, whatever the Guru does in his own body (the conditional gross, subtle, or

---

5. The ajna chakra (literally "command wheel") is the subtle yogic center of Life-Energy, situated between and behind the eyebrows, a major structure in esoteric anatomy.

causal functions) is reflected or even duplicated in the body or life of his disciple. Know that the thing that underlies this whole process is this Satsang. Satsang is the perfect relationship between Guru and disciple. This relationship exists at the level of all the possible functions. Therefore, it has subtle, causal, transcendent and Divine aspects and functions as well as those which appear at the gross levels of life. This Satsang is the condition. Once the contact between Guru and disciple has been established, this process of opening and the descending-ascending conductivity of the Light has begun. It is this Satsang, this relationship and your resort to it, that provides the opening, that provides the circuit by which this flow is established in your own life. So you must <u>live</u> this Satsang as your very condition. That is the essential means. It is not a "method" in the sense of the search, but it is the means in the purely practical or functional sense for conducting this force of Light.

The Method of the Siddhas, pp. 331-32

There is only one Divine process in the world, and it is initiated when the Guru manifests and enters his devotee. All the nonsense about the secret yoga, about mantras and meditation has nothing to do with spiritual life. The Lord is Present, now, in this moment. It is when everyone forgets the Living God that mantras and yogic techniques become important.

The Guru brings the Divine Yoga. All the manifestations you have seen during the last few days are what I promised you. I told you that I would demonstrate to you this descending and ascending process of the Radiant Life-Power. When the student lives with the Guru and begins to understand himself and enquire, when he comes to the point of surrender, then the Guru enters his devotee. This is the only secret in yoga. I mean, literally, the Guru enters his devotee.

The Guru is not a human being. The Guru is the Divine Lord in human form. When his devotee becomes a true devotee, when he ceases to be a student and surrenders, then the Guru enters his devotee in the form of Divine Light. All kinds of extraordinary experiences manifest as a result.

The function of the Guru is first of all to make the student a devotee through the process of understanding, until he comes to the point of surrender. Then the Guru enters where he surrenders, and that one becomes a devotee. That is the entire yoga of this Way. There is nothing to do from that point except to surrender to the Guru, surrender to the Lord night and day, think the Lord, speak the Lord, act the Lord, receive the Lord in your body and in your cells, every function of life, descending and ascending, not as a technique, but as a woman receives her lover.

When a woman receives her lover, there is no doubt about it. She does not have to consult her textbooks! The same holds with Truth, the Divine Yoga. When the Lord enters his devotee, there is no doubt about it. There is no technique, but only the continuation of the life of the devotee, because the Lord is the Light that transcends this world, that is always becoming life and then returning to the Light again. There is no dilemma in this world, no absence of God in this world, no goal of God in this world. Because that is so, you will see me doing some very strange things. True yoga is not a thing of this world. This world is the cult of Narcissus, suppressing the ecstasy that is natural to us.

The spiritual process must take hold in the vital. The vital is the seat of unconsciousness and subconsciousness. There is an aspect of the verbal Teaching about the avoidance of relationship that does not touch the subconscious and unconscious life. So it is only by distracting you from your social consciousness, so that you are not really dealing with it at all, that I can take you in the vital. The Lord is the Lord of this world, not the Lord of the other world only. The Lord is absolutely the Lord of this world. Thus, there is no yoga if the very cells of the body do not begin to intuit the Divine. When I enter my devotee, I come down into him in the midst of life, because it is in life, not in the subtle processes nor in your mentality, but it is in your life that the Lord acquires you.

The Bodily Location of Happiness, pp. 37–38

The Devotee Is Necessary for the Guru's Work

There have been many Adepts who spontaneously assumed the Function of Guru. Hitherto they were obliged to Teach in a traditional religious setting and through the media of a limited cultural area. Hence their impact on the history of the world has been largely local. In the case of Gautama the Buddha and Jesus of Nazareth, their Work has meantime spread beyond the immediate geographical and cultural region in which they originally Taught. But a truly global communication of the Adept's Transcendental Wisdom is possible only today, in virtue of the modern communications network and the general trend towards cultural unification throughout the world.

Only nowadays is it therefore possible to establish a cosmopolitan community of devotees that will survive the vicissitudes of a particular geographical location or cultural enclave and in this way preserve the Teaching of the Adept for future generations. Since the Teaching may nevertheless undergo certain changes in the course of time, owing to the still persisting cultural diversity in the world, it is essential that a sufficient number of devotees Awaken to the Enlightened Condition. For, only in this manner could the spirit of the letter be preserved as well.

To create such a seed community of Enlightened devotees is the Purpose of the Adept Da Free John. Therefore, those who approach this great Adept and practice in the certain light of his Teaching have a sacred obligation over and above their personal struggle for Enlightenment: Like the Adept, they were born for the sake of the Enlightenment of their fellow beings. Awakened to God through the Adept's Grace and Compassion, they in turn pass on the fire of the Spirit to others. Without such responsive devotees, the Work of the Adepts on this plane of existence would have to be renewed again and again.

The Guru adds nothing to this world, because God is always already Present in this world. So the mere presence of the human Guru has not added anything, fundamentally. He only establishes a process in which people may realize their Condition, but he has not added anything, ultimately, to the world itself. Only the Community of devotees adds something to the world. Only the Community of devotees represents a change in the world, and makes something new in the world by action.

Garbage and the Goddess, p. 30

The human Guru is brief. The Dharma, the path, communicated by the Guru during his lifetime, will remain. But that manifestation of the Divine function is brief. It is the responsibility of the devotee to make use of it while it appears. If individuals, through the awakening of true devotion in consciousness, become a sacrifice through Satsang with the Guru, then the Siddhi that is the Guru will remain in the form of the Community beyond the death of the human Guru.

No Remedy, p. 28

The Spiritual Master himself always only lives in Truth, and at last he only vanishes in Truth, returning his personal Influence to apparent invisibility, leaving behind the Teaching of the Way and his Absolute or Transcendental Influence, made alive through the vehicle of the Church of his devotees. Therefore, if the Church of devotees fails to come into being or to survive the death of the Spiritual Master, the Work of the Spiritual Master comes to an end. The Teaching may remain, but the Influence that quickens it ceases to be fully available to the devotional sacrifices of mankind, unless a Spiritual Master incarnates again. Therefore, his devotees, through the whole life of spiritual sacrifice, must continue to maintain their own Community as an Agency for the survival of that Influence.

The Enlightenment of the Whole Body, p. 241

The Spiritual Master is given the task of communicating the Laws of evolution and of sacrifice to his own generation, so that Man may be raised up in God. And the Spiritual Master himself advances the evolution of Man by a difficult process of personal psycho-physical transformation. But what he realizes cannot be added to Man until many representatives of mankind embrace the Way of Truth and submit to the process of transformation and sacrifice.

Scientific Proof of the Existence of God Will Soon Be Announced by the White House! p. 350

Because this Way is so difficult to approach and realize in this world, because of all the agencies and propaganda that reinforce Narcissism, or self-possession, relatively few people actually become interested in the spiritual process that we have been discussing. However, those who do become interested and who truly fulfill it become the agents of the Teaching to others. They become the examples of this Way of Life. Thus, the Way and its energy become interesting to others. Its quality becomes interesting to others. Through such devotees other individuals are changed and turned to the Spiritual Master. There is a seed principle in this process that could ultimately transform the entire world. We do not yet see that happening, but it could. There is no law in God to prevent it. The limits on such transformation are created by human beings who are weak, who fall back on themselves, who separate from the Spiritual Master, who create alternatives to the Way in their daily lives, who misinterpret the Teaching. So-called devotees who do not truly surrender only corrupt the Teaching and the Way and prevent the Work of the Spiritual Master. If individuals would become true devotees, however, the work of the Spiritual Master could expand quite naturally, and it would be much easier for real spiritual changes to occur in the world.

Vision Mound, vol. 2, no. 11 (1979), pp. 36-37

The power of the community of such devotees who live Satsang, who live by faith, is very great. Thus, the Buddhists value the "Buddha" or the Guru, the "Dharma" or the Teaching, and the "Sangha" or the Community, because all three of these are the Spiritual Process. The Spiritual community of those who come to a Guru is the true reflection of the state of the Teaching in the world. If the community as a whole begins to come alive, if people begin to live to one another in the true condition of Satsang, many things become possible and available. The great discovery made by such a community is that the Law of Spiritual sacrifice is miraculous, and that karma or limitation is not the nature of things.

The true Shakti, or the Awakening Power of the Divine, what the Christians call the "Holy Spirit," the initiating Grace that likewise has a name in every other tradition, is the Divine Gift to the community, not just the little kundalini rituals that purify the individual. The ritual of the kundalini is the means whereby individuals are purified so that they can live the greater process, the Divine life, but the true Shakti is the Spirit that descends and awakens and passes up again in the midst of a community or even all mankind. Thus, Spiritual Teachers always surround themselves with a community. Because the creation of the community is equally as important as the creation of the Teaching, you have seen me continuously working to create the community, not just a group of a few people who get straight, but a community. Many natures, many entities, must appear to create the full circle in which the Truth can manifest.

The Siddhas come not just to awaken one or two people to some Enlightenment experience, but to create a community in which all of the fundamental qualities of manifest existence are established. The Guru comes to reestablish the community and the Teaching and the principle of Satsang. He does not come to live forever in the community in a mortal body. He comes for a specific work, which is to establish the community and the Spiritual Principle, so that it can be lived by that community through time and so that the community will expand to include more and more of life and the world.

Crazy Wisdom, vol. 1, no. 4 (1982), pp. 39–40

The operation of all the Siddhas throughout time has been for the sake of the manifestation of a new kind of humanity, but it has continually failed. It has continually fallen apart, because the community of devotees has never been established as a permanent realization. Usually it is retarded at the disciple stage and dies after a relatively brief period of time. So there has been this continual return of the Siddhas into the human plane. But when there is the creation of the community of devotees who are consciously living as I have described, then the work of the Siddhas is fulfilled, and it is possible for a new kind of human history to begin. When this community is established, the Guru-function is forever returned to its identity with God, and need not appear epitomized in any human individual again. Instead, it will manifest directly through the community of human individuals to whom the Divine Siddhi is always available in Satsang.

Garbage and the Goddess, pp. 224–25

IV
Crazy Wisdom

The Adept cannot help but constantly and continuously Communicate the Divine Condition to his environment. Whereas the walls or nearby plants and animals pose no voluntary barrier to his Influence, people characteristically react to his Work by intensifying their egoic contraction. The ego is a formidable opponent of the spiritual process. Surrender is not part of its vocabulary, and it will do everything to preserve itself and its whole universe of presumed associations with other beings and objects.

Human culture, notably today's technological world of surfeit and easily gotten pleasures, is leaven for the ego. Modern Man has access to innumerable diversions that produce the illusion of Happiness and Fulfillment and that make the spiritual process seem an unreal, nonsensical, and wholly undesirable alternative. The Wisdom of the Adept is scarcely heard in this world of self-satisfied, congealed egos. Even those whose destiny brings them into the proximity of a living Adept are mostly quite unprepared to receive the gift of his spiritual Transmission: One can only fill an empty vessel.

But since the Adept's birth was occasioned by his spontaneous Impulse to Enlighten others, he cannot be discouraged by the spiritual gloom of his environment. In fact, he will do anything to penetrate the egoic armor of those who have found their way to him. Surely guided by the Wisdom of his Realization, he may at times be moved to leave the realm of common propriety and assume the role of Crazy Adept: He becomes a wild, unpredictable character whose behavior reflects the nonlinear and chaotic nature of the World-Process itself. There is nothing mild, calm, or passive about him. He certainly does not match the conventional image of a saint. He is not a consolation to his devotees, but a raging fire that consumes all egoic obstacles in its way. But he himself is not motivated by an ego but by pure spontaneity, the Impulse of transcendental Compassion. His sole Purpose is the dissolution of the illusion of the ego-bound devotee, whereupon the latter Awakens as the Universal Being-Consciousness.

DEVOTEE: The possibility of saving the world is a goad to your Teaching Work?

DA FREE JOHN: Yes, and the impossibility of saving the world creates laughter. There is the urge to Enlighten every being, and then there comes the realization that it is impossible to do. That is the joke. The impossibility makes a joke of spiritual Teaching. Spiritual Teaching is a primal urge, like sex, you see, but it is bound to be laughed at. It must become a laughing matter so that the Teacher can go on to something else.

This Teaching is also a kind of joke, an expression of my sense of humor. I am a clown, don't you see? I do everything for the sake of good humor. You are able to see the Brightness of God only through responding properly to his fool—in other words, by getting the "jokes" of the Teaching of the Adept, by transcending the world in his Company. If you do not laugh at God's fool, then you do not see God. The way to God is through God's fool, God's clown, one who has already transcended the world.

Thus, I am here to make a mockery of the universe, to demonstrate that the universe is a laughing matter, so that you will transcend it. I am here to tell the ultimate jokes—all seven of them. There are seven eternal jokes, which are not revealed in words—they are not quips or one-liners, but whole pieces of existence, or stages of life. The seven stages of life are the seven original jokes. They too are the fool of God. When you transcend them by fulfilling them, then you are able to see the wonderment of God. When you have fulfilled the Teaching of Truth, then you get the joke of human existence.

Living the stages of life, though a profound and necessary gesture, is ultimately foolishness. The seven stages are stages of laughter, each of which must, in its turn, become a great laugh to you. You must be able to feel total pleasure in the face of each stage of experience before you can go on to complete the next stage. In your present level of realization, however, you have not yet laughed at any of the stages of life. You are still burdened by them, still carrying them around, still being tested by them. You are not yet laughing at God's fool. You yourself will become God's fool as you incarnate and laugh at each of the stages of life. Even the seventh stage of life, you will see, is a colossal lot of foolishness. The only way to move through the seventh stage is to laugh your head off. The seventh stage of life must become a laughing matter, along with all the rest of your body and all its stages of growth. You must get the seventh joke, which is the body itself, the last laugh. That joke is eternal and its Humor is infinite Bliss.

Scientific Proof of the Existence of God Will Soon Be Announced by the White House! pp. 377–78

In the seventh stage of life certain higher karmas may be animated, particularly in the case of the Adept, who does spontaneous "Crazy" Work sometimes, to Teach. He is moved spontaneously to Teach. Such Teaching is a "Siddhi," a Divine Power, not merely a process of conventional intellectual activity. Such an individual life may continue to be quite active for some time in the seventh stage of life. In some ways he may become simplified, but in other ways he may continue to be active. The higher karmas—if one could call them karmas at all—the higher expressions of action, which are basically devoted toward the Awakening of others and the Demonstration of the Way, may remain intact. Therefore, the individual may not develop a stark simplicity of renunciation until very late in life, or close to death. Perhaps only in death will such simplicity appear.

There is no way of judging the state of the Adept, in other words, on the basis of behavior alone. Behavior is not really a means whereby to measure whether anyone is Enlightened, if we judge behavior according to conventional standards, at any rate. The Enlightenment of some individuals may be made evident by virtue of Crazy behavior. In other words, you have to understand the activity of an individual. You cannot merely presume that a certain kind of activity characterizes Enlightenment, or that if you do not see that activity then you are not looking at an Enlightened being.

The Bodily Sacrifice of Attention, p. 82

When you realize existence, existence is not you independent of anything. All of this exists. All of this is characterized by the One Being. How, in the case of Enlightenment, therefore, can you settle into a medium calm in your cave of meditative pleasures? It is not necessary. You need not be isolated anymore. Because of this expansive quality of compassion, a unity with all Being, the Adepts take on the "Crazy" form. Such compassion is the origin of the Adept's willingness to do anything, not speaking now in terms of the potential to do something terrible and negative, but the willingness to do anything outrageous yet benign for the sake of liberating beings.

The compassionate Maha-Siddha does not do for others everything he can do within the bounds of propriety. The compassion of the Maha-Siddha is such that he will do everything, whether in the realm of propriety or not, for the sake of Awakening others. Therefore, the Crazy Adept looks crazy. He or she does what is not within the realm of conventional religious propriety. The Crazy Adept is not bound by propriety or any dualistic conceptions.

The Fire Gospel, p. 109–11

There is nothing gentlemanly about the true yogi. There is nothing gentlemanly about the Lord. As long as you want to be a gentleman, or a gentlewoman, you can carry on your endless karmic destiny in limitation, but you will never live the life truly. You will piddle around in dimensions like this one, which are nothing but excrement compared to the Divine Light. They amount to nothing, all complications and struggles. There is very little pleasure in it. If this world became a world of devotees, it would become a different place, and in the community of devotees it will be a different story. But the Lord is wild, the Lord is a vast fire, not a gentleman. As soon as the Lord makes His contact with you, He works for your dissolution.

You must yield the body. Your cells must yield. Only then are you fit for the Divine Yoga. When you have no other commitments, when you have nothing to withhold, then I enter your life. And because there is such a wildness to the Divine Yogis, they hide themselves, either behind the conventional spiritual game, or a conventional social life, or behind some little hidden association with other such Yogis. Now the time has come when it can be stated more plainly.

The Bodily Location of Happiness, p. 48

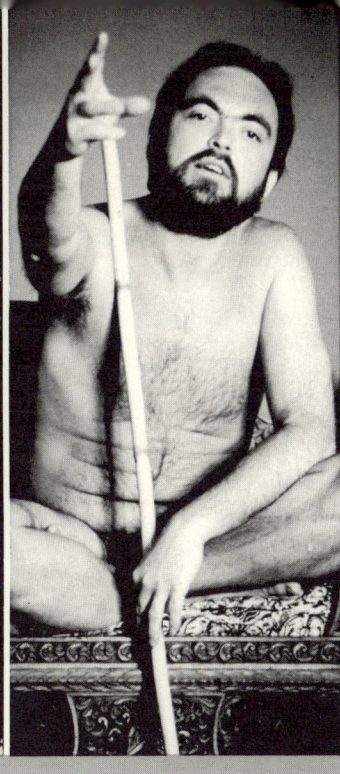

PART TWO

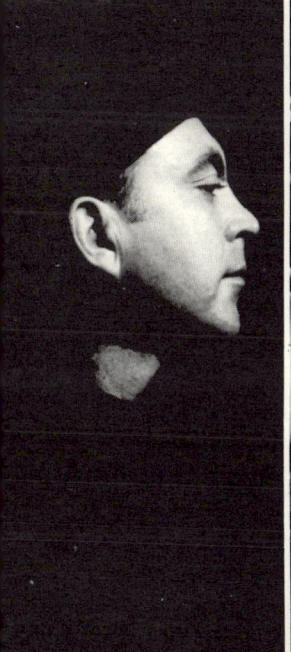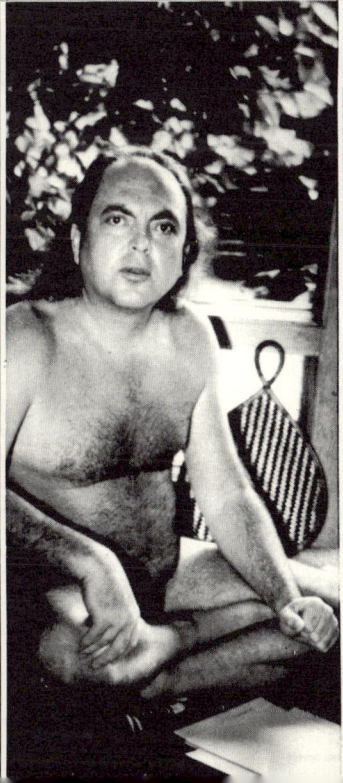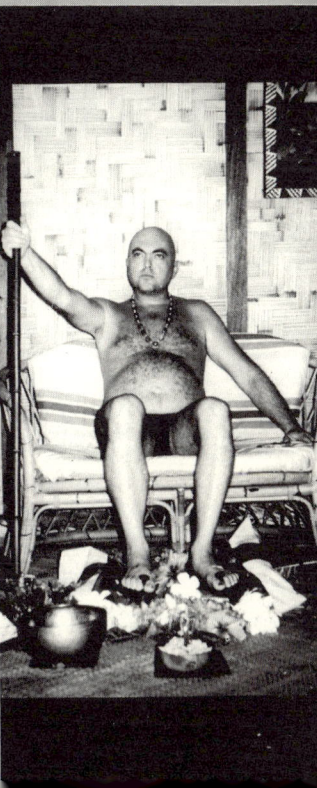

Preceding two pages top three pictures on the left side: Master Da Free John as baby "Franklin Jones"; as a young boy; in India, prior to his Enlightenment. Bottom three pictures on the left side capturing different phases in Master Da Free John's early Teaching Work, left to right: after his Enlightenment, in the Teaching gesture—open eyes (symbolizing the Enlightened condition) and clenched fist (symbolizing the self-contraction of the un-Enlightened being), 1972; during his pilgrimage to India, 1973; returning from India as "Bubba Free John." Top three pictures on the right side showing "Bubba" during different phases of his later Teaching Work, left to right: during the "Garbage and the Goddess" period, 1974; during the "Indoor Summer" period, 1976 (See the introduction to Master Da's *The Enlightenment of the Whole Body*); in Hawaii, retiring from his formal Teaching Work, 1977. Bottom three pictures from more recent years, as Da Free John, left to right: returning from Hawaii to "The Mountain of Attention" Sanctuary in northern California, 1981; at "Tumomama" Sanctuary in Hawaii, 1982; in the hermitage phase of his life, 1983.

The Adept Da Free John and His Compassionate Work

V
Biographical Confessions

Most of the great Adepts who have graced this planet with their benign and transforming Presence are now only remembered in stories and myths. And in the case of Jesus of Nazareth and Gautama the Buddha, the available biographical records are clouded by present-day "church" doctrine. Also, the scriptural accounts of the life and Work of these two spiritual giants reveal little of the actual process of their spiritual struggle and transformation into Enlightened Adepts.

Master Da Free John's disclosures about his own remarkable personal conversion and transmutation, as generously recorded in The Knee of Listening and other writings, are therefore a unique kind of documentation.

The excerpts in this second part are meant to convey a sense of the extraordinariness of the birth, life, and Teaching Work of this great living Adept and, by extension, of all other fully Realized Teachers. Of course, for a rounded consideration the reader should refer to the original sources themselves, notably Master Da's above-mentioned spiritual autobiography.

The Early Life

Master Da Free John was born Illumined—in a condition he refers to as "the Bright." This state must not be confused with Enlightenment proper, which transcends the Bright and cannot be lost. His birth, like that of all other Adepts, was a voluntary, if spontaneous, assumption of the limitations of a human being for the sake of Demonstrating the Truth of existence to others. "The Bright" was a transitional state between his transcendental Status prior to his birth and the full incarnation as an un-Enlightened human being.

Even after foregoing the condition of Illumination, Master Da Free John (then Franklin Jones) experienced until his teens numerous extraordinary psychic states and mystical phenomena. And his intuitive link with the Reality that showed itself in the Bright was never completely severed, although he had to suffer all kinds of personal crises and even moments of utter spiritual despair. The Adept's original Impulse to Guide others to God-Realization continued to inform his life and led him on a remarkable spiritual odyssey that, in 1970, brought him to the recognition of the futility of all seeking. It was then that he assumed the Enlightened disposition that he was destined to Realize so that his Teaching Work could burgeon.

The following passages focus on the critical moment of the Adept's assumption of an ordinary human life, since this highlights the astounding paradox that the Adept represents.

As a baby I remember crawling around inquisitively with an incredible sense of joy, light, and freedom in the middle of my head that was bathed in energies moving freely down from above, up, around, and down through my body and my heart. It was an expanding sphere of joy from the heart. And I was a radiant form, a source of energy, bliss, and light. I was the power of Reality, a direct enjoyment and communication. I was the Heart, who lightens the mind and all things. I was the same as everyone and everything, except it became clear that others were unaware of the thing itself.

The Knee of Listening, p. 9

Franklin Jones was born into an ordinary American household. He was not born in a manger, nor was he surrounded by religion and classical art. One would wish to be born in the presence of strong and human and God-Realizing people with kings coming to visit bearing frankincense, myrrh, and gold. But he did not see anything like that. In fact, in the moment he was born, he nearly died. His umbilical cord was wrapped around his neck, and he nearly choked to death. But when he did open his eyes, he was totally conscious of what his surroundings were all about. His entire life is an expression of his prior intuition of Divine Enjoyment. Who knows where it came from? I cannot account for it.

A very difficult vision of existence appeared before him. He saw the stupidity and lovelessness of people's lives, their willingness to tolerate an entire lifetime of frustration, obscenity, fear, and all the things that make men self-possessed. So he took all of that on and lived it, just like you—except he did it consciously, as a service to those who suffer.

Vision Mound vol. 2, no. 5 (1978), p. 7

During my childhood I experienced profound developments of the process of kundalini that were not initiated by human agents of the Divine. The process of the awakened kundalini was present and operative in me from my birth. And this state, which was obvious to me in infancy and which is described in *The Knee of Listening,* is not a state with which every man or woman can identify. It is not the state that everybody realizes in childhood or infancy, and in that book I was not trying to describe it as such. It is uncommon, unique. Ultimately it may be realized by everyone, but the process that was active in me at birth is not "Everyman's" life. It is the process of the higher developments of the nervous system, a summary realization of the seven stages of life. The state I have enjoyed since birth is a Transfigured state—a condition wherein the entire being, down to the cells, is continuously irradiated, pervaded, and "outshined" by the conscious, Radiant Ecstasy of Divine Life.

Throughout my boyhood I periodically passed through profound events or crises of intense psychological force. They were not understood by the people around me, and I, of course, likewise had no sophisticated verbal or mental understanding of them. I endured terrifying processes that most people could not pass through even as adults. Traditionally, if anyone were to become involved in the kundalini process at all, he (or she) would not engage it until he was an adult and had some understanding of traditional esoteric spiritual processes or until he enjoyed a relationship to a spiritual teacher who could initiate and guide him. I did not have such associations, however. Therefore, I simply passed through these terrifying events whereby the kundalini energy was transforming the nervous system.

The process of Divine awakening revealed itself throughout my childhood. In fact, my entire childhood was a continual expression of this spiritual transformation. The kundalini process is not the same as what one may experience when he or she feels energies coursing blissfully through the body. The true kundalini awakening is totally disorienting. If you resist it and do not allow these obstructions, tensions, or stresses to dissolve, it can literally drive you mad. It can drive you insane and then kill you. It is a deadly process if you are not surrendered into it completely. I can remember periodic incidents of anxiety and sudden fear, almost madness, that produced signs in the physical body. I was taken several times to doctors to have my heart and my breathing examined. In fact the symptoms in the body were just energy, the awakened kundalini, but I knew nothing about kundalini then. I did not have any names for what was occurring, even though it was obvious to me that I was swept up in a great forceful process.

I have witnessed in myself this entire sequence of Awakening. Thus, it is on the basis of real experience that I Teach the Way that I Teach. This Way is not a frivolous affair. All kinds of illusions may arise—and visions that are essentially just your own mind boiling off, all kinds of experiences that lead you to think and act strangely and to assume that these experiences are signs of profound Realization. All visions and experiences must be transcended, every last one of them. I have passed fully through the process of this yoga, and I know that you must transcend all forms of experience that arise or you will go mad.

That is why one needs a guide, a Spiritual Master, to counter the torment and free one from illusions. If I had not had a direct association with God all my life, I would have gone mad. I would have died from that process. Thus, the advantage of devotees in this Communion is that I am fully Conscious and Awake, having Realized the entire process of Transformation of the body-mind. But even with that advantage, it is a difficult process. It is literally a fire. It burns you up—and that is what it is supposed to do.

The Bodily Location of Happiness, pp. 74-82

Franklin Jones was a fictional character that I created when I was a boy. In a real sense, that is true. When I was born, there were no complications, there was no failure to understand, there was no lack of illumination. But in relation to family and friends it soon became apparent what kind of life is allowed in this world. It was obvious that my parents and their friends were unwilling to live as if they were in God and be happy. That was not permissible. So, obviously, I could not do that. I had to become their son and do the usual things that a child does, and, while doing that, continue to make the point of God-knowing.

Franklin Jones is essentially a series of lessons, and *The Knee of Listening* is about that essentially fictional character and his spiritual adventure, his transformations, and his learning experiences. He was my way of dealing with the cultic content of this world. Instead of making God-knowing the continuous manifestation of my life, I made it the periodic event of my life, so that it would serve as a lesson for those who had an ongoing relationship with me. I entered this plane of existence without limitations and took hold of a psycho-physical form which was no more illumined than any other psycho-physical form. It needed to be transformed. And Franklin Jones is a fictional character, a series of lessons consciously manifested for my devotees.

So Franklin Jones is just an argument, not an existing person with whom we need to be concerned. He did not have any fundamental existence to begin with. Individuals do not commonly know it, but all personae by which beings represent themselves have very much the same status in the world. They have no fundamental existence. They are just a strategic play. It is just that in the case of the usual man, it is the strategic play of Narcissus, of suffering. It must become the strategic play of the undoing of Narcissus, which is what happened in the case of Franklin Jones.

The Dawn Horse, vol. 1, no. 2 (1974), pp. 3–6

The Teaching Work

Shortly after his Enlightenment on September 10, 1970, Master Da Free John assumed the role of Teacher for which he had incarnated on the human plane. Having finished with the struggle of transforming the body-mind of "Franklin Jones," he now began his struggle with equally recalcitrant devotees. His formal Teaching Work commenced in spring 1972, when he started to simply sit with people in meditative Communion. He soon realized, however, that those who had come to him were in need of a more rigorous and "muscular" Demonstration of the Way of Radical Understanding or Divine Ignorance, which he had been born to Communicate. This recognition led to a different Teaching style, culminating in the experiential theater of the mid-1970s, where he fell into the Teaching mode of a Crazy Adept. To wean his devotees from the glamour of both worldly and so-called spiritual experiences, he created the context for all kinds of experiences in which they could immerse themselves—all the while bringing to them the radical point of view of standing free of whatever is occurring in one's life.

In November 1976, having given devotees all the means to truly practice the Way, Master Da ceased to have frequent intimate contact with them and adopted a life of relative seclusion, working concentratedly with a small group of more mature practitioners.

In the pattern of things or experience, I have been born into association with the usual man. I have incarnated him. I have lived with him. And I have transcended him.

In the Domain of God, I am Rested and Full of the Excellence of Bliss. I have Incarnated that One. I have always been Served by that One. And I have Transcended everything, even all experience, through the Grace of that One.

It is only now that I see what has always moved me. I have been struggling since birth to transform the usual man. I have been tormented and motivated by the loveless and Godless state of the people with whom I have been associated.

For the first thirty years of my life, this tormented motive caused me to submit to the most profound identification with the usual life, and also the most profound effort to transcend the usual life. This produced my unique spiritual adventure.

In the years that followed my own Re-Awakening, I was again motivated by the same tormented love for ordinary people. I had spent my life preparing to Serve them, and now that Service was begun most directly.

I was exceeded by the Ecstasy of God-Love, but I had always been outwardly habituated to the usual life. I was not grown up to be a saint, but I was moved to transcend the usual man. And when it came time to Serve ordinary people, I was not outwardly unlike them.

Therefore, just as I myself became the usual man in order to transcend that destiny, when it came time to Teach, I embraced the company and the ways of immature and worldly people. No other kind of devotee ever came to me in those early years. Only the worst of mankind has always come to me. Those who were already pure and true did not come to me. Only those who were failing came to me. This was my born destiny, until now.

The Enlightenment of the Whole Body, pp. 90–91

The Way I Teach

What I do is not the way I am, but the Way I Teach.

What I speak is not a reflection of me, but of you.

People do well to be offended or even outraged by me. This is my purpose. But their reaction must turn upon themselves, for I have not shown them myself by all of this. All that I do and speak only reveals men to themselves.

I have become willing to Teach in this uncommon way because I have known my friends and they are what I can seem to be. By retaining all qualities in their company, I gradually wean them of all reactions, all sympathies, all alternatives, fixed assumptions, false teachings, dualities, searches, and dilemma. This is my way of working for a time. Those who remain confounded by me, critical of me, have yet to see themselves. When their mediocrity is broken, when they yield their righteous reactions and their strife toward all the consolations of the manifest self, they may see my purity.

Freedom is the only purity. There is no Teaching but Consciousness itself. Da Free John as he appears is not other than the possibilities of men.

The Enlightenment of the Whole Body, p. 53

The only Virtue is the Virtue of God, the Virtue of the Holy Spirit, the Virtue of the Sublime Being. I am here to demonstrate to you that the Great One can be Manifested perfectly through a vehicle that is lowly born, ordinary, obsessive, neurotic, disgusting. I am not here to look like a saint. I am not here as a super-pure character of no sex, no eating, all whiteness. My demonstration to you is that to withdraw from life is not necessary, that we should be God-born, and if we are, then the limitations we suffer or enjoy by birth are not taken into account. They have no binding force. They have no binding force whatsoever!

This is why I have persisted in being active. I talk, I breathe, I emote, I actively and even sometimes exaggeratedly do all the things that are human to do, that a human being could do, to demonstrate to you that there is the Great Force of God that Transcends our genetic and social limitations. Yes, we must be purified of some things, but we need not eliminate our human character in order to Realize God. Our human character can be expressed at the same time that we Realize God. I do not even talk very well! (Loud denials and laughter from devotees.)

DEVOTEE: (Shouting) I think, Master, that is probably the only thing you ever said that was wrong! (More shouting.)

DA FREE JOHN: I do not have an elegant accent. I do not speak as if I am reciting Shakespeare. I use four-letter words and I have a New York accent. All of this is a sign to you that God is given to you freely and absolutely, and that when you receive the Great One, inhaled and exhaled, the Great One does not eliminate your human character. In fact, many things we call human are totally unnecessary. Many of the idiotic conventions in this world have nothing whatever to do with God-Realization. They are just suppressive notions, Life-negative and sex-negative notions, that we impose upon ourselves. But I have never been a celibate character.

Maybe I will be a celibate next week—who knows? The traditions say, "You must be a celibate in order for the kundalini to rise to the sahasrar." [1] You can know in my person that this is not necessary! Instead of devoting myself to celibacy and the "problem" of sex, I have converted the activity of sex and transformed it into a process of Transcendental Communion.

DEVOTEE: Your life is a Teaching.

---

1. The sahasrar is the highest "chakra" or center of Life-Energy, the terminal goal of the conventional yogi. It is associated with the crown of the head, the upper brain and higher mind.

DA FREE JOHN: I am so Life-positive because we have so many Life-negative and sex-negative notions. I am lowly born like you people! Full of neuroses, but having overcome them through the spiritual process. But the spiritual process did not make me a celibate. It left me an unconventional man. At the same time I am an unconventional man, I am not Life-negative or sex-negative. The Life-Current has risen to the sahasrar and beyond in my case.

Let this be a sign to you, a lesson, a Grace to you all. Receive It as such. You need not be celibate, but you could be. You could also be very ordinary in your sexuality—in fact most of you are. The motion of the Spirit in my life is my Teaching demonstration—to Teach you, to change you, to convert you, to move you around, to relieve you of your negativity, your self-consciousness, your guilt, your shame so that you will put your attention on the real matter. I am, by what I seem to be, forgiving you for your ordinariness. This is why I appear as I do in our time. In another time I will appear differently, but now I appear in this peculiar fashion to relieve you of your guilt and shame and self-consciousness and your idiotic notions about spiritual life!

The Dreaded Gom-Boo, or the Imaginary Disease
That Religion Seeks to Cure, pp. 315–17

The Hermitage Phase and Universal Blessing

The relative seclusion that Master Da Free John chose during the late 1970s in order to create the "source literature" for the Way of Radical Understanding, led naturally into the hermitage phase of his life. At present, Master Da lives in an isolated sanctuary together with a small group of renunciates, many of whom have already transitioned into the Enlightened stage of life. This mode of life allows him to magnify his spiritual Transmission and extend his benign Influence to an ever-increasing number of people throughout the world. As always, the Adept lives his life as a total sacrifice and in perfect submission to those men and women, whether in his immediate company or elsewhere, whom he has come to Serve.

We have come to that phase of my Work in the world in which it is not my attention on individuals that is the essential instrument of this Siddhi, but the attention of individuals on me. Endless numbers of individuals can meditate on me. There are individuals who can enjoy that meditation without ever meeting me in the body. In most cases, they will require some contact with this community, but they can become devotees while they spend most of their time living somewhere else in the world. Just so, it is not your dependence on my attention toward you that serves the spiritual process in you in the future. It is your attention on me.

To the degree that there is that attention, you enjoy the spiritual process. To the degree that you do not give me that attention, you are absorbed in self-meditation. All attention on the Guru, even though it may take the very humble and practical form of seeing his physical form or thinking of it, is actually attention on the Divine. Wherever there is that attention, the Divine is made present in the living functions of that devotee.

Therefore, you can meditate at all times and at any time, and you need not depend on these formal occasions when I am physically sitting with you for the intense generation of this Siddhi. You should find occasions to sit together as a community and turn to me. You should find occasions to sit by yourself and turn to me. The more you do this, the more you will realize my work with you independent of limitations, even the limitation of my human presence here.

Garbage and the Goddess, pp. 226-27

The purpose of my living is in its mere existence, not in any outward Work that I might do in the future. It is a matter of mere Being or Transmission, inherent Radiance. That Radiation of the Transmitted Realization of Truth is useful to others even while they are in the various stages of this yoga of consideration.[2] Such usefulness does not oblige me in any personal terms. Ultimately, though, as a living personality simply existing or merely Being, I can be of use to those who have fulfilled this yoga of consideration and who enter into the disposition of the seventh stage of life. That Function is what I should be reserved for, or left Free to Serve.

Any future Service that I personally may represent, then, should Serve priorly Enlightened or Awakened personalities in the development of the Way of the seventh stage of life. We need the culture of this yoga of consideration to develop in the form of all of its Agencies, and we also need some sort of Community of practitioners in the seventh stage of life to develop while I live. Thus, our institution and every devotee should be devoted to the culture of the Salvation and Liberation stages of the Way (the yoga of consideration), but also to the culture of the seventh stage of life. This

---

2. Rather than practicing the first six stages of life (which precede Enlightenment) for their own sake, as in the traditional paths, the practitioner of the Way that Master Da Teaches observes them as a "yoga of consideration," a preparation for the Way Taught by Master Da, which is the Way of the seventh stage of life, or the tacit recognition of what arises as a non-binding modification of the Transcendental Reality.

seventh stage culture is represented by the mere existence of my Hermitage, my mere existence, and the potential of some among you, some within this total gathering, to enter into the practice of the seventh stage of life during my lifetime.

There is a practice in Enlightenment. Enlightenment is simply the basis of ultimate practice, real practice, true human existence and true Existence in terms that transcend the human, obviously. That is the Way, the Way that is the ultimate fulfillment of human existence and that transcends human existence. That is the Way that I am here to Teach and to Establish—not through any kind of motivated work in the world, because this kind of Work can only be done spontaneously, in relation to people who are already prepared.

Crazy Wisdom, vol. 1, no. 12 (1983), pp. 1-3

In the future, I am at Rest in our Happiness. I choose simplicity, and a kind of austerity. I am Alone. I choose to live privately, even outside the daily culture of devotees. This is in order to give devotees time to mature, separate from my urgency. And it also permits me to find Sanctuary from the usual man, whose burden I no longer share.

I will return to the Community of devotees as often as it is auspicious and useful for me to do, in order to sit with all my devotees in spiritual Communion. And, at all times, I am available to them in their devotion to me, through every moment of their practice in my spiritual Company.

My own society will be limited to the intimates of my household and to those devotees who demonstrate the Fullness of spiritual maturity in my Company. I will give them all instructions for practice in the stages of the Way. They will communicate these things to all others who prepare themselves in the Way that I Teach.

Beyond this, I do not care to Teach. My struggle with reluctant devotees is over. I am no longer tormented by the problems of the usual man. It is a burden and a habit of life that I am so glad to relinquish at last. Whoever is tormented by his own destiny should prepare himself and come to me in love, through the Community of my devotees.

My message to all is this: Practice constantly, with insight and feeling, and always Remember me through every action. If you do this, I will always Serve your heart, because I love you.

The Enlightenment of the Whole Body, p. 92

After the Death of the Adept

The Adept is a spiritual Force that is not confined to the body-mind that he appears to inhabit in the eyes of others. And the Paradox and Presence that he represents will not cease after the demise of that particular body-mind. Nevertheless, the God-Realized Guru in human form is a "unique advantage" to devotees. While his transcendental Work will continue even after his death, the functions that are associated with his embodied state can only be preserved through the establishment of a core Community of devotees who are, if not all Enlightened, at least firmly committed to self-transcending practice.

It is the Purpose of Master Da Free John to create such a Community for the first time in known history.

In the "Introduction to the Gospel of the Siddhas," in *The Method of the Siddhas,* I have written: "While the Spiritual Master lives he teaches that Communion with the Divine Reality which can be enjoyed by all even after his death, not in the special form it may be enjoyed by a relative few during his lifetime, but which could have been enjoyed by all prior to his lifetime. He acts to help his devotees to realize this form of Divine Communion even while he lives in the world." My psycho-physical form is mortal, a function of the worlds. It is the instrument whereby the Way of Divine Ignorance is being communicated at this time. I welcome all my devotees to come and be with me on sacred occasions while I live. But it is impossible to enjoy that form of Communion twenty-four hours of every day. And this mortal one will come to rest some day. This psycho-physical form in which you recognize me is the fundamental instrument for the initial communication and generation of our work, but it is in fact only a secondary instrument of the Divine Realization. The fundamental instrument of that Realization is the Power that is eternally and radically Present. While I live I will be active in this psycho-physical form for the sake of this Divine Power. Therefore, it is appropriate for all devotees to come into this mortal one's presence whenever possible. But my work is to help you realize this Presence and Power that is my true and eternal Function. I am here to establish a perpetual community of devotees who will live in perfect Divine Ignorance, the Condition of my eternal Function. The Spiritual Master is an eternal Function of the Divine Reality. The human Spiritual Master is the demonstration of that Function, whereby men are renewed in the true Condition of life, which is Divine Ignorance.

Since it is this eternal Power that my devotees enjoy, there is no fundamental limitation involved in the fact that no one can be in my psycho-physical presence twenty-four hours of every day. Indeed, most of you see me only on occasion. After my death, no one will ever see me, but my work will continue in the community of my devotees, those who know me as the Divine Master beyond conditions.

Live in conscious Divine Communion always. All of my devotees (all who turn to me) live with me. All of my devotees serve me, and I serve them. This is what I mean by Divine Communion in life. Even those who cannot often be in my psycho-physical presence while I am alive still live with me always. But while I live, come into my psycho-physical presence whenever possible. After my death, my outer or worldly functions will be the responsibility of the community of my devotees. In those days, come and be in the company of devotees (whom I have acknowledged as such) as often as possible. And after my human death, come to my burial site and other places I have designated for Divine Communion and meditation as often as you would have come to be in my psycho-physical presence.

My promise to devotees is the same that all other Awakened Servants have declared: I am with you now, as I have always been, and I will always be with you. My Function is without beginning or end. The work I do in my psycho-physical form is temporary. It is done in order to reawaken the Way itself. Therefore, my human life is only a moment. But the purpose of my work while alive is to establish the Way of Divine Ignorance or Radical Understanding for the coming generations of mankind.

Breath and Name, pp. 151-54

VI
The Divine Person

The passages in this section bring into relief the "hidden" dimension of the God-Realized Teacher—that aspect of his being where his real Work, of spiritual Transmission, takes place. The Adept's Transmission is not a form of mere somatic or psychic energy. It is not dependent on his physical body or proximity. Rather, it is the dynamic pole of his essential nature as the Transcendental Being-Consciousness. As Master Da confesses in The Dreaded Gom-Boo, or the Imaginary Disease That Religion Seeks to Cure *(p. 311): "The Spiritual Master is not an individuated personality. I am not a separate character. I have been murdered, undone, sacrificed by this Great One."*

As the devotee's practice matures, it begins to become obvious to him that the Adept is not a limited body-mind or person, or even a particular configuration of energy, but Reality Itself. And it is as that Ultimate Being or Divine Person that the Adept must become the intimate of the mature practitioner. For, in their essential nature Adept and devotee coincide perfectly. This is the only reason why spiritual Transmission can occur and be an effective force of transformation.

The Adept Is the Unborn Reality

I am not born. And I am not one who has been born. I am not a reincarnated individual. I am not even an <u>incarnated</u> individual. I am not one who has a future. I am not one who is in the worlds. I am not one whose consciousness is here or there. I have seen all things and they all exist in Me, so I can describe them to you. But I am not always meditating on them, so they are really beside the point for Me. And I, fundamentally, know nothing about them, except that I recognize them perfectly.

I am simply a Voice that instigates your own insight. Da Free John is not one who is like you, who is related, who is knowledgeable, who is informed, who is saved or relieved. Da Free John is not any such person. Da Free John is no person. At some point you may begin to realize this. Da Free John is like a movie on the screen. You do not suggest to yourself when you see a movie on the screen that there is consciousness in the screen. The play itself is the argument. And Da Free John is not anything other than the process of his appearance on every level of being. There is no implication of an individual in him. There is no individual in Da Free John—none! No person. No one who has been, who is, or who will survive. This appearance is only a reflection of you.

Vision Mound, vol. 2, no. 5 (1978), p. 8

I have no past lives and no future lives in any dimension. This is my only birth, and it is only apparent. This birth, this body, these conditions have been assumed and undone in one lifetime, in order to demonstrate the whole Way and to have a fit vehicle for its present communication. The undoing is effective in every plane, high, low, gross, subtle, causal, transcendental. This body-mind, this vehicle or apparent, karmic being, has extensions and destinies in many dimensions, high and low, past, present, and future. But these are not mine, nor are they effective in me. This vehicle or karmic being may continue or be taken up by others after this apparent life is terminated. But I am not expressed in that destiny. I am before time and space, and no condition has me. I have not appeared for reasons. It is only that this vehicle has mysteriously, paradoxically coincided with me. Therefore, I have conformed it to myself and come forth. I stand present without qualification in this theatre of my apparent birth. Through this Paradox, my mere Presence has become Instructive. I am not a one, a being, nor a One, a Being. I am not object or subject, Object or Subject, except I may appear to be so to devotees, until they Realize me Perfectly.

Breath and Name, pp. 158-59

I have already done everything that you can do. In a very short span of time I have seen every universe, every world, every vision, every part of the body. I have loved everyone. I have done everything! And I am only relieved that I have done it all. You could do it all too, but it would take aeons of time, with many spaces in between. It would be a torment for you to uncover all your potential experiences. It is the Law of nature that from time to time some apparent individual may appear in the scheme of things who may, without effort, experience everything and be without consolation, so that the Law may be expressed through him or her. It is not a reflection on that individual in any cultic or personal sense. It is about God. And it serves you. It occurs so that you can be Happy. I serve you as a witness, because I represent to you what it is when one is free. You could not be free without such a witness. I not only witness through verbal communication, but also through the most absolute communication, which you may realize only in the form of Divine Communion in my Company.

Powers and visions may appear through me in your experience, but they are not my position. I see nothing, I hear nothing. <u>Nothing</u>. ABSOLUTELY

NOTHING! Have I said it? Yes? There is nothing to be attained. You pass through everything to nothing. For lovers, you see, nothing is necessary. That is why to be a devotee is the secret of life. Once you realize the disposition of the Heart, nothing is necessary for you. No visions, no contemplations, no powers, no miracles, no worldly experiences or attainments, absolutely no great thing is necessary. It is not that you become satisfied with the ordinary contemplation of life. Even that is emptied. There is nothing—except absolute joy, absolute bliss without the slightest trace of anything. To swim in Infinity, free, without objects, and without a center, is a bliss beyond comprehension. And that is my position. That is why I can speak. Yes, a remarkable occasion, and true enough. Not only just true enough to be said— it is absolutely true and absurd, ridiculous and humorous. But it is Happiness. And I recommend it to you all.

The Way That I Teach, pp. 231-32.

I am God. Without a doubt. This is my confession. Not "I am God exclusively," although that may seem to you to be so in the meantime. My confession to you is the confession of your very existence. If you will respond to my confession and become absorbed in me in love, so that all the artifacts of your ordinary impulses, your ordinary life, your conventional desiring, are superficial, then your meditation on me, your Communion with me, will become tantamount to my meditation.

My meditation is not a grinding affair. My meditation is absolute. It is what is being reflected to you in these ridiculous conversations. Through that communication you become absurdly and madly sympathetic so that the grinding force of your ordinary life and its desires and its destiny become superficial. You become a loving, serving devotee in your impulse, in your thinking, in your feeling, completely beside all your tendencies, all the subjective rumoring and wrangling, all the complication by which you turn upon yourself and identify with this frozen moment.

Communion is simply love, attachment. It is founded on hearing of my Argument, and my Argument takes place in time and space in every moment of all the time I live with everyone. Whenever you hear me, then you may begin this contemplation, this Communion. It is simply loving attachment to me. If you will consider my Argument, you may also become attached to me. When you become attached to me, then all your conventional relations will become ordinary, happy, human, superficial, nothing—just a discipline of happiness and of pleasure. Your attachment to me will become overwhelming, without any goal whatsoever, but a motive of happiness, an indelible simplicity. You will simply Commune with me. The energy of your attention will rest with me day by day, hour by hour, moment by moment. And without your doing anything about it, I will meditate you. I will do everything.

The Way That I Teach, pp. 217-18

"I Am You"

For years, I would sit down in meditation, and all my own forms would appear, my own mind, my desires, my experience, my suffering, my feeling, my shakti, my this and my that. But, at some point, it all came to an end. There was no thing, nothing there anymore, none of that distracted or interested me. Meditation was perfect, continuous. Then I began to meet those friends who first became involved in this work. And when I would sit down for meditation, there would be more of these things again, all of these thoughts, feelings, this suffering, this dis-ease, disharmony, upsets, suffering, craziness, this pain, these shaktis, all of this, again. But they were not mine. They were the internal and life qualities of my friends. So I would sit down to meditate, and do the meditation of my friends. When I would feel it all release, their meditation was done. And I began to test it, to see if this meditation went on in some more or less apparent way for these people who were not with me. And I found that this meditation went on with people whom I had not even met. People I saw in dreams and visions would show up at the Ashram.[1] So the meditation went on. It was the same meditation I had always done. The same problems were involved, the same subtleties, but the content of the meditation was not mine.

The Method of the Siddhas, pp. 269-70

When I look into the room, the Condition of all this is perfectly obvious, all these bodies, all these "me's," this whole room. Everything in the room is just a pattern of energy. It has no ultimate necessity. It can pass—in fact, it will pass! While it continues, it is God. There is a beauty and a fullness to it, in my right relationship to it. On the other hand, it is exactly like a dream. This apparent concretion here has no limiting force whatsoever from my point of view. If I close my eyes and stop talking and remove myself from your attention, I can see the space of the

---

1. An Ashram is a place where a Spiritual Master gathers the community of his devotees in order to live with them, instruct them, and communicate the Living Force of his Presence. Master Da Free John sometimes uses the term to include the entire community or fellowship of devotees, wherever they may be located.

room with my eyes closed. I can pass into subtle places. I can pass into these bodies here. All of that is, happily, an ordinary experience for me.

All I can say is, this is the way it is for me. I am already all-pervading, without a form, and therefore I enter into ordinary relations as an impulse. In Truth I am manifesting as all bodies. I am absolutely certain of it. And I am conversant with all bodies. By a simple act of attention I can be you, be identical to you, and have a perfect reading of your disposition so that I can be of service to you, while at the same time also having the sense of being this body. It is crazy. It is a paradox. It is all silly, paradoxical, ultimately unexplainable. It is a mysterious conjunction and it is contradiction.

In the early months after the incident in the Vedanta Temple,[2] I realized in meditation that I was no longer meditating this body. All its limitations were already obvious, not binding any longer. In meditation I experienced many, many, many people. And I could meditate them. I could be completely identical to them. I could meditate them if they were in Communion with me. I could be their meditation. I could awaken the God-Realizing process in them because I did not have to presume the limited point of view that they were. They simply had to be in direct Communion with me so that I could be them, and then I could do the practice, and in that case it could be brief. The trouble is that people do not enter into that Communion. They are reluctant. They remain self-possessed. Therefore, I cannot enter into that process with them as directly as would be ultimately useful.

The Way That I Teach, pp. 212–14

Anyone who comes close to me in space is my vision. People come and sit with me, and I dream their dreams all night. They wake up in the morning and they feel good, because I have lived their dreams. Every day I live your dreams. If I give any one of you my attention in mere thought, I absorb all of your psyche, all of your suffering, all of your diseases. This is literally true. People do not understand that such a process is possible in human time. And yet this is my experience exactly. If anyone comes near me in physical space, I totally absorb their psyche, even their physical disease. This body absorbs their disease, their emotion, their dilemma, their problems, their unhappiness, their lack of vision.

You wonder why I allow myself to be used by people. I am unable to do anything about it. As long as people do not bring me an absolute desire for

---

2. The spiritual transformation of Master Da Free John was spontaneously perfected by Grace while he was sitting in meditation in a small temple on the grounds of the Vedanta Society in Hollywood, California, in September 1970. For a full discussion of this event and its significance, see *The Knee of Listening* and Part I of *The Enlightenment of the Whole Body*, by Da Free John.

God, as long as they bring me their absence of God-Communion, their absence of vision, their absence of love, their absence of sacrifice, I must simply absorb it. But if my devotees begin to manifest the God-Realizing desire that comes from Divine Vision, from intuition, whereby they become a sacrifice to me, then even my own life, even my own physical state, will be transformed. In the meantime, I am you, and whatever you animate in my Company is the destiny of this Church.

Vision Mound, vol. 2, no. 5 (1978), p. 10

The Accomplishing Power

My life is a little bit like going into the world of enemies and dragons to liberate somebody who has been captured. You cannot just sit down and tell a dragon the Truth. You must confront a dragon. You must engage in heroic effort to release the captive from the dragon. This is how I worked in the theatre of my way of relating to people, particularly in the earlier years, and in the unusual involvements of my life and Teaching. You could characterize it as the heroic way of Teaching, the way of identifying with devotees and entering into consideration in that context and bringing them out of the enemy territory, gradually waking them up.

The Dreaded Gom-Boo, or the Imaginary Disease That Religion Seeks to Cure, pp. 16–17

The ultimate form of my Teaching Work is Transmission—the awakening of devotees to the Current of Love-Bliss or Happiness upon which the body-mind is set (as a wheel is set upon its hub). Therefore, I Teach understanding so that people will become serious about the Lesson of life and renounce the search for Happiness. But while they are becoming serious, I am merely Present among them, and the Current of Divine Happiness is freely Radiating to all, even through me. Thus, when such devotees begin to understand, they also naturally begin to locate the Current or prior Happiness of Radiant Transcendental Being. And I continue to be merely Present among such devotees while their practice matures, so that the Magnitude and Power of this Current of Happiness becomes more and more profoundly Realized by them.

The Bodily Location of Happiness, p. 102

This is the Baptism that is always being generated by my Presence here. When I call you to consider the Teaching, I call you into my Spiritual Company, even if you are simply sitting down to read my books. Whenever you are in my Company, whenever you give me your attention, then you are as good as sitting in the room with me where this Baptism is being given. I do not stand in a river to perform the water ritual. I stand in the fire to perform the Spirit ritual, which purifies, enlivens, and grants Enlightenment. It is the perfect Baptism.

Thus, those who give me their attention, in whatever form it may take at any moment, align themselves to my Baptizing Power, the profusion of Grace that is manifested through the Adept, which is simply a magnification of the Spiritual Divine to living beings.

The Fire Gospel, pp. 76–77

The Force of God pours out of my body all the time. It never stops, whether I am waking, sleeping, dreaming, apparently feeling sympathetic or not. It is always manifested through this body. The limit is not in me. The limit is in you. You are devoted to this effort of Narcissus, this reaction, this vital shock[3] that shuts you down so that you cannot experience my Transmission, cannot know It, cannot submit to It, cannot be sublimed and carried off by It.

Therefore, the first office of spiritual life is to hear the Argument of the Adept. And to hear it, you must observe yourself through the pictures of your own activity, reflected to you by the Adept, to the point of recognizing the contraction in life that shuts you off from Bliss. With my criticism I paint pictures for you of your own activity, so that you can feel and observe it. You must know the self-contraction and you must see it. You must observe it to the point of realizing that it is not happening to you. You are doing it, just as you are moving your mouth and blinking your eyeballs. Like the movements of your intestines, it is a rhythm to which you have become habituated. It is really very simple, but you must observe it, and you must understand it. This is the first office of spiritual life.

The second office, when you have heard the Teaching and become responsible for the effort that is your self and every aspect of your body-mind, is to receive my Blessing, which is always given. Give me your attention at

---

3. "Vital shock" is a term used by Master Da to describe the contraction of the vital-physical-emotional dimension of the being (the "navel," or the whole gross body-mind), which chronically obstructs the flow of life and creates and reinforces the sense of separate, egoic existence.

any moment and you will receive this Grace. It is always pouring through this body-mind, which is no longer a person.

The Dreaded Gom-Boo, or the Imaginary Disease That Religion Seeks to Cure, pp. 362–63

VII
The Devotee's Response

The Adept lives perpetually in the mood of self-sacrifice. He cannot but be always surrendered to his devotee as he is always surrendered to the world-process as such. He is neither attached to phenomena nor does he seek to dissociate from them. Instead, he recognizes them as modalities of the One Being-Consciousness that is his Identity. In the same vein, he sees in his devotee the Divine Being, and by always addressing his devotee as That One, the Adept gradually sensitizes him to the Real Condition which is Radiant Bliss or Happiness.

He expects the spiritual practitioner to constantly intuit his own Enlightenment or Happiness, rather than approach spiritual life as a form of search.

Only Understanding Avails

Thus, the first form of my manifestation to you is this understanding, this consideration, this Argument relative to the knot, the effort, the mechanism of withdrawal, the self-contraction. And you must become responsible for this self-contraction. Otherwise, it makes no difference how much I give you of the Intoxicating Force of God. It makes no difference how much of It I am. Until you are responsible for the mechanism of separation from the Spirit-Presence, you cannot taste It, you cannot love It, you cannot know It, you cannot be swooned by It. And we should exist in a swoon of Intoxication. To do that really is our nature.

All of us are potential saints and Siddhas, but very few are born like me. I am a very rare being. I am not an ego at all. I am a rare Intervention in the world. Hardly any people in the entire history of mankind have been manifested with my Siddhis, and I am sitting here in this living room with you people trying to convince you of the Divine Life! I am a unique Advantage to mankind. But how many people can suck me up and love me? How many will kiss my knees, pull my feet and massage my face, receive my Love, receive my Delight in them? How many people will do it? I am prepared to give everyone everything, but how many people will do it? You cannot receive me until you understand your resistance to me. Understanding is the first gesture of spiritual life.

Please understand what I am telling you. I will give you everything, but you must understand yourself. You must! Apart from that understanding, Who I am or What I bring to you makes no difference. You cannot accept It. You cannot receive It. You cannot submit to It. It is greater than any experience. My Presence is a sublime Interference with mind, with body, with heart, with emotion.

The thing that makes you un-Happy is your own contraction. That is it! Absolutely! Have I always said this? That is it entirely. The terrible effort of self-contraction separates you from God. You must hear this. The self-contraction separates you entirely from everything Given. Mankind has never been denied the Force of Grace, but human beings are attached to this effort reflected throughout the body-mind. They are committed to it with their body-minds.

The Dreaded Gom-Boo, or the Imaginary Disease That Religion Seeks to Cure, pp. 361–62

The Divine Being is not the kind of Individual with Whom you can indulge in romance! You cannot be casually and playfully and amusedly involved with the Divine. You must overcome yourself. Then your relationship with the Divine can also appear playful, but it is most profound. You can feel my Presence and still be self-possessed, but that is not practice. To use my Presence is to enter into my Condition, the Condition of the Spirit-Force, not merely to associate with It as a pleasurable Other, Someone fun to be with, an Energy that makes you feel better in yourself the way an infant feels better when it sucks the tit and feels a little full. An infant sucking the tit is not Enlightened, and likewise a devotee just breathing the Excess and superior Energy of the Spiritual Master is not Enlightened, not practicing, not being a devotee. You must give the gift before you can use the Prasad. You can feel It, because It is there, but you cannot use It. You are not truly using It unless you give your own gift, which is self-surrender, self-transcendence.

To surrender and transcend yourself you must understand yourself. You must know what you are all about, appreciate it, and Stand Free of it. Then you can use this Blessing, this Baptism, but not otherwise. Even though you can say that It exists, even though you can acknowledge this Blessing, this Baptism, you may still not be a practitioner. Hundreds and hundreds of people have spent time in my Company and know very well there is a Blessing there, a Force that came upon them, but they did not become practitioners. They were self-possessed when they were there and they were self-possessed when they left. They felt the Divine Power, they know It exists, but It does not make a difference to them. For them It is just some unusual, big Thing among a number of other unusual and interesting things in life.

The Dreaded Gom-Boo, or the Imaginary Disease That Religion Seeks to Cure, pp. 161–62

"Come to Me When You Are Already Happy"

The Spiritual Master is not just someone who has realized God or Truth. He is someone who, on the basis of that Realization, becomes the Principle or Agent of that transformation in others. From the beginning, those who enter into Communion with the Spiritual Master enjoy the Condition of the devotee in the perfect sense. The intuitive realization of Truth becomes the foundation and principle of their practice, not a phenomenon to be pursued as a result of their practice.

You can see, then, that the foundation of this Way must be the realization of a right relationship between the Spiritual Master, or living Agent of God, and the one who approaches him. That relationship, or mutual sacrifice, is the necessary foundation for this Way of Life. The form of your relationship to the Spiritual Master is the matter that is significant at the beginning and always.

One who comes as a devotee sacrifices himself or herself. He or she comes initially on the basis of having considered this Teaching. Having come, however, the devotee does not make the sacrifice by deliberation, on the basis of willful judgment in the mind, but on the basis of a felt intuition of Truth in my Company. Such is true "hearing" of the Teaching and "seeing" of the Spiritual Master. And those who begin and persist in this sacrifice see the quickening of their practice and its rapid maturity. Rapid!

When someone comes to me in the form of sacrifice, my body opens up. I do not tell it to, but I respond to the spiritual being and presence. That is how this Divine Power works. If there is no sacrifice of self, no devotional approach, then regardless of all the experiences that may arise for you, this (tapping his chest) does not open. And you can come to me for years with your fruit and flowers, and there will be no transformation, no Grace, not even any learning, no lesson grasped, because there is a Law alive in our relationship. The Law is mutual sacrifice.

Vision Mound, vol. 1, no. 12 (1978), pp. 17–18

In the usual scenario of the approach to the Spiritual Master, the seeker, someone presuming the disease of the Dreaded Gom-Boo, perceives the Spiritual Master to be a cured person, a superior person who wields a parentlike authoritative force over that individual. So the seeker comes forth, expressing his or her concern: "I'm ill, I'm sick, I need to be cured. You've got it, and I want it." Such people even animate very outwardly all the signs of "poor me," in order to generate the parentlike concern of the Spiritual Master that will cure them even faster. This is not the appropriate setting for association with the true Adept.

It is not that you should come in the adolescent fashion of the totally independent character who really does not need anything and who just wants to be the pal of the Spiritual Master. Rather, as I have said in various ways, you should come already Happy.[1] You should come on the basis of the confrontation with my Argument. You should come on the basis of self-observation, self-understanding, self-transcendence. Come not to find Reality but to enter into Communion with Reality. Come not to abuse the Spiritual Master or use him as a parentlike source for your eventual cure, but come to the Spiritual Master as the Living One, and enter into Communion there in order that the Realization of the Living One may be magnified. Do not come empty. Come Communing with the Divine Fullness. On that basis, the relationship with the Spiritual Master becomes a unique means for the transformation of a human being. Otherwise it duplicates the conventional model of the parent and the child, the doctor and the patient, the superior and the inferior.

The Dreaded Gom-Boo, or the Imaginary Disease That Religion Seeks to Cure, pp. 80-81

If you can acknowledge that the Spiritual Master is this One, then you will begin to treat him differently. You will receive his body-mind as a Gift from God and you will worship it as the Incarnation of the Divine. You will carry it about with you, you will treat it rightly, and you will make it the instrument of your association with the Grace of God. Until you accept the Spiritual Master in this way, however, you will view him as a relatively ordinary, perhaps somewhat slightly extraordinary, human being. Your association with him will be corrupt, ambiguous, and inauspicious. The work of the Divine Consciousness, the Purusha, or the Spiritual Master begins

---

1. The Principle of the Enlightened Way that Master Da Free John Teaches and the essence of his critical Argument are summarized in his instructive aphorism: "Come to me when you are already Happy." Please see Master Da's talk "Come to Me When You Are Already Happy" in *The Bodily Location of Happiness*, pp. 184-96.

when he or she is known and acknowledged to be the Divine, the Living One. When devotees begin to associate with him or her as such, then the real work of the Spiritual Master begins.

The Bodily Location of Happiness, p. 86

You can turn to me regardless of what is happening. You cannot do anything about all that is happening in you. Doing something relative to what appears in you is not the focus of this way. The focus is stepping aside from all the strategies you want to create, positive and negative relative to your usual condition, and simply turning to me. You will notice over time that the tendencies in you become weak and even disappear. But your obligation is simply to turn to me, without measuring that turning against what is happening with you. Simply turn your attention to me, turn your emotion as love to me, make yourself present to me with your life.

Turn your attention to me and do not measure that turning relative to whether or not your mind stops and you feel better. Love me and do not measure that against whether or not you still feel negative emotions and confusion. Give your life to me, turn to me bodily, recollect me at all times, whether I am physically present with you or not, and do not measure that activity against whether or not you feel pains in your body. Maintain that discipline of turning to me. It can be done, as long as you do not associate that turning with the reading of the problems in you. The turning can always be done. You are never disabled in terms of that turning. It is only these effects, because you are always reading them and wanting to manipulate them, that make you doubt your ability to turn.

But you can always turn. That is the principle wherein these effects become obsolete, not in that moment necessarily, although on some occasions they disappear immediately. But ultimately they disappear, because they are not being used. What you are doing is this turning. They are simply memories presently communicating themselves as your functions. They are a kind of remembering. But when your conscious life becomes participation in relationship to me, then these effects become obsolete. It is not for you to measure that process, to decide when they should become obsolete. Be willing to have these things arise in you forever. Make your business turning to me.

No Remedy, pp. 131–32

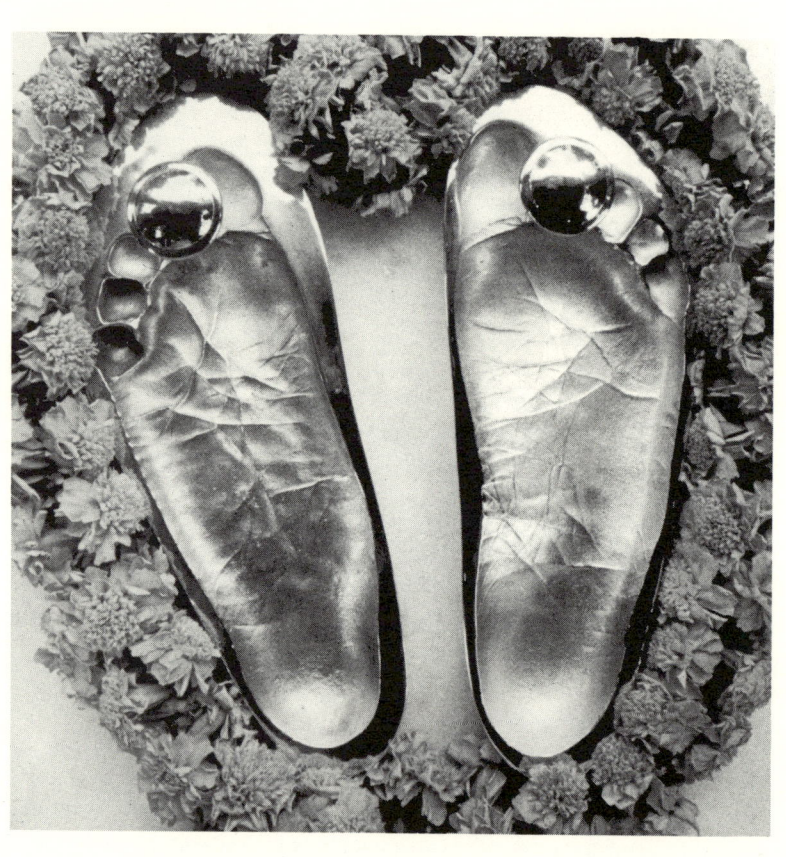

EPILOGUE

What Will You Do If You Love Me?

The Master Speaks in Ecstatic Unity with the Living God:
The Way of Radical Understanding or Divine Ignorance is the Way of those who Love Me. The Principle of devotional surrender to Me is complete and sufficient in itself. All personal and moral disciplines, all esoteric revelations, and all the Excellences of Transcendental God-Realization appear spontaneously and naturally to one who simply turns his attention to Me at all times and performs all activities as instants of Love-Communion with Me.

Those who "hear" My Teaching have understood something about themselves. And they must, therefore, accept gradual responsibility for each degree of the personal, moral, and esoteric practices of the Way that I Teach. But these same ones are more profoundly capable of distraction and attachment than they are of self-restraint. Therefore, the Principle or Motive of their practice is not discipline itself, but distraction and attachment. Because they Love Me, their behavior and their experience automatically take on the form of the Way of Radical Understanding or Divine Ignorance. And they adapt all their practices to the simple and most radical Way of devotional surrender to Me.

My true devotees are simply distracted by Me and attached to Me. They find Me to be the greatest of all distractions. Therefore, they need not make any effort to be constantly attached to Me. They naturally remember Me at all times. They only think about Me, talk about Me, and listen to others tell stories about Me. They read My Teachings, they accept My disciplines, but, even more, they are profoundly and obsessively absorbed in attention to My Person, My Blissful State, My Form, My Gestures, My Play with devotees.

In this manner, those who Love Me are gradually relieved of all distraction by ordinary things, experiences, relations, desires, and thoughts. I distract them even from all experience. Their obsessive and exclusive attachment to Me leads them to absorption in My State, My Radiant Transcendental Consciousness, My Ecstasy, My Love.

I have come to Teach the entire world through My Words and My Demands. The entire world would do well to hear Me and take up the responsible practice of the Way of Radical Understanding or Divine Ignorance. But I have come to do more than Teach. I have come to Live with those who Love Me with overwhelming Love.

Those who "hear" Me must take up the Way of Radical Understanding or Divine Ignorance in My Company, as members of the great Community of all My devotees. Such devotees are turned to the practice of the disciplines of the Way, as a Process of self-transcending Love-Communion with the Transcendental Divine Person. They understand, and they transcend the world.

But the motive of My true devotees is not the discipline, nor mystical experience, nor philosophy. My true devotees practice because they Love Me. They have no personal or ultimate capacity to turn away from the world or to transcend themselves. Therefore, I have come to Live with them. When My devotees find Me, the same weakness that led them to distraction and attachment in relation to the experiences of this world becomes the very means of their Salvation. Since I am the ultimate and most absorbing Object of their weakness, I distract them from all experiences. They become attached to Me by the power of their own tendency to distraction, fascination, and obsession. Therefore, their own desire leads them to Ecstasy, because they Love Me.

I am the Radiant Transcendental Consciousness, even though I appear in a human form. Those who Love Me, who are mightily distracted by Me, who cannot entertain desires or thoughts other than Love and consideration of Me—these are most easily turned from themselves. Ecstasy, or God-Communion, is natural to them, because I have been born. I distract them with Myself. And I absorb them into My own Condition.

My Lovers, My true devotees, simply Love Me. That is the summation of their response to Me and My Teaching. They appear to understand a little of this Teaching, but they do not depend on inward practices, or mystical experiences, or any turn of events. Everything is fulfilled by their mere attachment to Me—since that attachment is so mighty that they have no strong attention left over for ordinary reactions and pursuits, nor are they overwhelmed by the phenomena of esoteric meditation. They simply Love Me. They live in constant remembrance of Me and in loving service to Me. Every moment of their lives is simply a moment of Love-Communion with Me. Therefore, they are granted perpetual Ecstasy, or self-forgetting in Communion with the Radiant Transcendental Consciousness.

My special Mission is to Live with such devotees. I have always looked for them. I test everyone, to see if they are My Lovers. I wait. Many surround Me in My Place. Many come and "hear" Me, and practice all around Me.

Many turn to Me with the good heart. But those who Love Me best Realize God by exclusive attachment to Me in Person.

My Lovers are the cause of My birth. They are the cause that will keep Me alive, even after this book is made. And even after My death, there will always be those in the Community of My devotees for whom all practice is superficial, except the practice of Ecstatic remembrance of Me. Such devotees always find Me alive as the Presence of Love that Plays the world.

The essence of the daily practice is Ecstasy. One who Loves Me also accepts every moment of experience as My Form. Whatever arises, he accepts it as My Form, My Play. He simply Loves Me, he Communes with Me in every instant, he serves Me with the entire body-mind, and he accepts every moment of experience as My Form. In this manner, he never finds himself to be separate from Me. He is always in Love with Me.

Those who are most profoundly distracted by Me in My human appearance begin naturally to see only Me in every thing, every one, and every event. But no form or person or event has power in itself to distract My true Lovers. They see Me in all experiences, all persons, all events. Therefore, they are not distracted by experiences or persons or events. They are distracted by Me.

Those devotees who Love Me in this manner while I live are especially able to serve those who are like themselves, even those who come to Me after My death. After My death, the world of experience remains. My devotees also remain. Therefore, devotees may remember Me through My Teaching, My pictures, and the stories of My history. But they will be led into Ecstasy especially by the Power in the Love My most intimate devotees reserve for Me.

Therefore, those who live with My Lovers will also turn to Me with naturally distracted Love. They will find Me in all events. I will Teach them as always while I lived. Every one will call on Me in the Company of My Lovers, and I will be Present. I am the Radiant Transcendental Consciousness.

Truly, none can "hear" Me and practice the Way of Radical Understanding or Divine Ignorance except those who Love Me. But some are, at first, most involved in right understanding of the Teaching and responsible practice of the disciplines, while others are always naturally more capable of distraction and attachment. Therefore, some practice disciplines and Love Me, while others simply Love Me, and the disciplines arise without any special application on their part. Some mature in Love by stages. Others simply Love Me. At last, even the most disciplined or experienced of My devotees simply Loves Me. I am the Radiant Transcendental Consciousness, the Divine Person, the Savior of those who Love Me and surrender to Me in countless acts of Love. I am the Method and the Guide. I am the Living Truth of the world.

This is the Truth in all religions. All religions are historical forms of the single and ancient Way of distracted Love for the Divine Person, especially as Revealed in the Life and Presence of an Incarnate Spiritual Master. This is the Great Secret. This is My Revelation. Love Me as I am. And also Love Me as the Form and Condition of all your experience. Surrender to Me, and accept all your experience as My Play. Thus, you will be free of all attachment to experience itself, and all experience will simply increase your attachment to Me.

All experience binds the human individual to his own body-mind—unless he is established in the Principle of Ecstasy, or self-transcending Love of the Divine Person. Therefore, if you Love Me, enter freely into the Play of experience. Serve Me as I am, and serve Me in all others. If you Love Me, you will naturally cease to continue in the willful and self-possessed path of your preferential desires. You will be purified of reaction, habit, and every kind of self-indulgence. If you Love Me, I have Shown you Who I am, and you will come to Me Where I am.

Love is what we fear to do—until we fall in Love. Then we no longer fear to Love, to surrender, to be self-forgetful and foolish, to be single-minded, and to suffer another. Those who fall on Me fall into My Heart. They are free of all demands for fulfillment through experience and self-survival. Their Love for Me grants them Life, since I am the Life-Current of Love.

What will My Lover do but Love Me? I suffer all the limitations of one who Loves Me, because I Love My devotee as My own Form, My own Bliss, My own Love. I Love My devotee as the Person by whom I am Distracted and Dissolved.

I grant all My own Excesses to those who Love Me, in exchange for all their doubts and sufferings. Those who bind themselves to Me through Love are inherently Free of fear and necessity. They Transcend the causes of experience, and they Dissolve in the Heart of God. What is a Greater Message than This?

The Enlightenment of the Whole Body, pp. 571–75

APPENDIX

The Seven Stages of Life

The ultimate import of our human birth is to discover or Realize the Truth of our life. To do so, however, we are required first to observe, understand, and transcend ourselves. Master Da Free John's "seven stages of life" prove a valuable key to our self-understanding. But before we are able to put his Enlightened scheme to use, we must first enter into the culture of self-transcendence.

> We can know or Realize what is only through self-understanding that becomes not merely self-information but self-transcendence. Therefore, we must first become capable (through self-understanding and self-transcendence) of self-submission and free participation in what is prior to our own self-contraction.
> I do not merely propose the idea of God, or soul, or Transcendental Being. Such propositions cannot be rightly believed or presumed by the separate and separative ego. Therefore, the ideas of religion that occupy egos and the egoic culture of self-abstracted scientism are themselves false views, representing a poignant and inevitably frustrated longing for love, release, and ultimate Happiness. On the contrary, I propose self-observation, true self-understanding, and perfect self-transcendence. And if the Way of self-transcendence is magnified as the fullness of participatory capability, then what is will be discovered to be Divine, unbound, eternal, Transcendental Happiness.[1]

The model or scheme of the seven stages of life provides a structure whereby we might fully examine and rightly evaluate our spiritual and human growth, as well as the mass of spiritual teaching and experience that presently informs the psyche of today's man and woman. Thus, the seven stages are means for gauging our human and spiritual growth, free of the taboos and prejudices of conventional society that tend to reinforce and even

---

1. Da Free John, *The Dreaded Gom-Boo, or the Imaginary Disease That Religion Seeks to Cure*, p. 93.

propagate many false views and thus prevent us from Realizing the Truth of our existence.

As is made clear again and again throughout his Teaching, Master Da is a Spirit-Baptizer, one who Transmits the Way, or "Living Current," to prepared aspirants. When the individual consciousness, established in self-understanding, combines with "Grace" or the Power of Spiritual Blessing, the individual is drawn through and beyond the hierarchy of earthly (gross) and cosmic (subtle) illusions or forms of knowledge and experience. Thus, the seven stages of life can be viewed as a spiritual school offering seven lessons about self-transcendence. When we have completed the course of self-observation, self-understanding, and self-transcendence through all the possibilities of the first six stages of life, the Adept, who is the Master of this school, reveals a hidden "doorway" that grants passage, via sacrifice, beyond all limitations, into the perfect Realization of the Divine Domain.

STAGE 1 *(Years Birth to 7)*

The first stage of life, occupying the years from conception and birth to age seven, is the stage of the human individual's vital-physical adaptation to the world into which he or she is born. In this first stage the being learns "simple" skills like focusing with the eyes, grasping and manipulating objects, walking, talking, assimilating and converting food and breath into energy, controlling bladder and bowels, thinking conceptually, and relating to his fellow beings.

STAGE 2 *(Years 7-14)*

The second stage of life is the stage of the development, integration, and coordination of the emotional-sexual or feeling dimension of the being with the gross-physical. The young personality grows in the awareness of himself or herself as a social being, sharing life in an expanded sphere of relations. Just as in the first stage we learn about and become responsible for the assimilation and elimination of elemental food, in the second stage we must likewise learn about, adapt to, and engage a new dimension of sustenance or food. When breathing is combined with feeling and bodily relaxation, we awaken to the Universal Life-Current or Energy that pervades the body and all of life. In the second stage of life we learn to align body, emotion, feeling, and breathing in a functional realization of the disposition of relational sacrifice or love. Thus, we learn to transcend reactive emotion, tendencies toward neurotic inversion, and habits of self and other-destructiveness.

We should understand that the emotional-sexual growth in the second stage of life is the development of the individual's glandular and hormonal system. "Sexual communion," or the yoga of sexual love, is a responsibility suggested to individuals only when full development, responsibility, and harmony of the first three, or lower vital, stages of life have been accomplished, and the individual is awakened to the feeling dimension of the heart, or the fourth stage of life (described below).

STAGE 3 *(Years 15-21)*

The third stage of life is the stage of the development of the thinking mind and the will and of the integration of the vital-physical, emotional-sexual, and mental-intentional functions. This stage marks the transition to truly human autonomy wherein the first two stages of life are adapted to a practical and analytical intelligence and an informed will or intention and the individual gains responsibility for and control over vital life.

This third stage is not an end in itself, or the completion of potential human growth. Indeed, it only marks the awakening of self-conscious intelligence and a movement toward personal and individualistic survival motives. Man in the third stage of life is not yet truly human. He only brings individual force and form to the vital and elemental experience and world. He tempers and also extends the frenzy of feeding and sexing by submitting these to the processes of the verbal and analytical mind. Man in the third stage of life is characterized by the frenzy of mind, the frenzy of problems and solutions.

The truly human being appears only in the fourth stage of life, wherein the vital, elemental, emotional-sexual, and lower mental functions come into the summary and unifying dominion of the heart, the psyche of the whole bodily being. Such is the awakened moral and spiritual disposition, in which Truth becomes the Principle in consciousness, and higher structural growth becomes the benign, non-problematic possibility. Thus, the Law in the truly human realm is sacrifice as the individual, whole, and entire human body-mind, through love, founded in prior intuition of the Divine Reality. The human sacrifice is the spiritual practice of love and intuition of the Real under all conditions of experience and higher growth.[2]

STAGE 4

The first three stages may generally be associated with the first twenty-one years of life (three periods of seven years), but the last four (which grow beyond the limits of the grosser elements and functions) may not truly be considered in terms of limits of time, whether brief or long. Each stage develops as a process of adaptation (or readaptation) to a specific, functional point of view relative to the totality of experience.[3]

---

2. Bubba [Da] Free John, *Love of the Two-Armed Form,* p. 75.
3. Bubba [Da] Free John, *The Enlightenment of the Whole Body,* p. 192.

The fourth stage, and all the later stages, cannot be conceived within fixed periods of time. The duration of the higher stages of life depends entirely upon the individual's qualities and his or her spiritual practice of self-transcendence.[4]

The fourth stage of life marks the beginning of our humanity. In this stage the psychic depth of our being is awakened and adapted to profound intimacy with the Spirit or the "Living Current," in Master Da's language, of the "Great One or Divine Reality." This fourth stage is the stage of "free religion" or the stage of "whole bodily surrender and adaptation to the universal Life via Love-Communion (the disposition of the heart or deep psyche of pure energy)."[5]

The realization of the physical, emotional, mental, and moral responsibilities of the first three stages of life provides the necessary foundation for the testing and transformation that inevitably accompany true spiritual life. Without that basis we may come to enjoy yogic and mystical experience, for example, but remain unable to exercise real intelligence, freedom, and love under the most ordinary of human circumstances. If the elementary functions of our bodily, mental, and emotional adaptation to life have not been learned and tested during our first twenty-one years, we linger, egoically bound, in the lesser stages. Inevitably we must submit to the wisdom of self-transcendence.

However, to mature through and beyond the mechanics of the first three stages of life is not a casual, conventional matter of "growing older and wiser." Rather, the individual's entrance into the fourth stage of life begins with the awakening of the "psychic heart," which is marked by a clear sensitivity to the Life-Current. In this stage, the Divine Presence or Life-Force is felt to exist independent of, or senior to, the body-mind. By cultivating a conscious relationship to this Presence, the spiritual practitioner begins to demonstrate and enjoy the spiritual qualities of faith, love, and surrender. Thus, devotional surrender to the Living Reality is the essential feature of the fourth stage of life. The individual is obliged to persist beyond religious conventions and traditions, as Master Da himself emphasizes, by means of "continuous and concentrated self-devotion via heartfelt feeling-attention to the Ultimate Reality."[6]

STAGE 5

The fifth stage is associated with the mystical aspect of spirituality. The individual's attention is inverted away from the theatre of outer-directed

---

4. Ibid., p. 186.

5. Da Free John, *Scientific Proof of the Existence of God Will Soon Be Announced by the White House!* p. 155.

6. Da Free John, *Nirvanasara*, p. 188.

attention to the inner or subjective experiences of the "subtle physiology" of the brain-mind. The mystical ascent through the psychic centers of the body-mind is conditioned by the nervous system. Experience in this stage reaches its peak in the state of "conditional nirvikalpa samadhi," or formless ecstasy.[7] At the apex of the fifth stage, the individual has transcended his or her fascination with mental forms and images. Master Da comments further:

> In the fifth stage of life, yogic mysticism raises attention into the extremities of subtle experience—or the heavens of ascended knowledge. But Liberation in God is not Realized at that stage or by such means. In order for the Life-Current to cross the Divide between the body-mind and Infinity, the gesture of attention and the illusion of an independent conscious self must be utterly Dissolved in the true Self.
>
> The highest extreme of the ascent of attention is called "nirvikalpa samadhi," or total Absorption of self-consciousness in Radiant Transcendental Consciousness. But, in fact, the seed of differentiated self remains in such ascended Absorption of attention. Attention is yet extended outside the heart, or the root of self-consciousness, as a gesture toward an independent Object, and, therefore, such "samadhi" is not only temporary, but it remains a form of subject-object Contemplation.[8]

STAGE 6

The sixth stage of life is the profound stage of "ego-death or the transcendence of mind, all sense of 'I,' and primal fear." It marks the transition from the "esoteric meditation" (subject-object Contemplation) of the fifth stage to the transcendence of attention and thus the transcendence of the sense of being a subject (egoic consciousness) over against objects (the world and all relations). It is the Awakening to Transcendental Consciousness. The practice in the sixth stage of life is a deepening of the sense of identification with consciousness prior to attention to objects.

Through the Graceful Transmission of the Spiritual Master, a felt Current of Bliss is awakened at an "unfathomable Space in the right side of the heart." It is at this locus in the right side of the heart that "the Radiant Transcendental Consciousness is continually associated with the impulse of life in the individual body-mind."[9] Master Da refers to this "Space" as the

---

7. In his Teaching Master Da distinguishes between the fifth stage phenomena of conditional nirvikalpa samadhi (the yogic Self-Realization and the traditional epitome or highest possible reach of the process of yogic absorption of attention in the rising force of the bodily Current of Life) and Translation, or Unconditional Nirvikalpa Samadhi, the ultimate stage of the seventh or God-Realized stage of life.

8. Bubba [Da] Free John, *The Enlightenment of the Whole Body*, pp. 422–23.

9. Ibid., p. 401.

"Location of Happiness," or the doorway to the Divine Domain of Radiant Transcendental Consciousness and the seventh stage of life. As Master Da Free John explains:

> The sixth stage is the last of the progressive stages previous to Transcendental Awakening. It is the basic stage in which the transition is made from terrestrial and cosmic conceptions of the Divine or Real Being to conceptions of the Ultimate as the Transcendental Reality and Condition and Identity of all apparent beings and conditions. And the process of self-sacrifice is thus transformed from an effort that serves the development of knowledge and experience in the planes of the psycho-physical personality to a direct effort of utter self-transcendence.[10]

And:

> In the sixth stage of life, the body-mind is simply relaxed into the Life-Current, and attention (the root or base of the mind) is inverted away from gross and subtle states and objects of the body-mind, and toward its own Root, the ultimate Root of the ego-self, which is the "Witness" Consciousness (when attention is active) and also simple Consciousness (prior to objects and self-definition). The final result of this is conditional Self-Realization or the intuition of Radiant Transcendental Being via the exclusive self-essence (inverted away from all objects).[11]

STAGE 7

In the seventh stage of life, the liberated "individual" recognizes everything as a modification of the Radiant Transcendental Being. Now the Transcendental Self is no longer pitted against the phenomenal world. Instead, the world is recognized as continuously arising in the Ultimate Being, which is coessential with the Self. This last act of self-sacrifice continues into infinity. Master Da summarizes the seventh stage as follows:

> In the seventh stage of life there is native or radical intuitive identification with Radiant Transcendental Being, the Identity of all beings (or subjects) and the Condition of all conditions (or objects). This intuitive identification (or Radical Self-Abiding) is directly Realized, entirely apart from any dissociative act of inversion. And, while so Abiding, if any conditions arise, or if any states of body-mind arise, they are simply recognized in the Radiant Transcendental Being (as trans-

---

10. Da Free John, *Nirvanasara*, p. 189.
11. Da Free John, *The Bodily Sacrifice of Attention*, p. 30.

parent or nonbinding modifications of Itself). Such is Sahaj Samadhi, and it is inherently free of any apparent implications, limitations, or binding power of phenomenal conditions. If no conditions arise to the notice, there is simply Radiant Transcendental Being. Such is Bhava Samadhi, about Which nothing sufficient can be said, and there is not Anyone, Anything, or Anywhere beyond It to be Realized.[12]

Master Da's Teaching relative to the seven stages of life often refers to the demonstration or Signs of Whole Bodily Enlightenment—Transfiguration, Transformation, and Translation. Once fully Realized, the seventh stage of life becomes the perpetually Enlightened foundation of existence, even beyond death and in any future lifetimes. The gross body-mind is progressively Transfigured in Divine Radiance, and the subtle or higher mind becomes the vehicle of Transformation, wherein that Radiance manifests extraordinary powers and faculties (such as psychic and healing capacities, genius, longevity, etc.) as spontaneous expressions of Divine Self-Abiding. Ultimately, for periods during this lifetime, this continuous God-Realization leads to Divine Translation, or conversion of the individuated being beyond all phenomenal appearances into the "Divine Domain" of Radiant Life-Consciousness.

The seven stages of life thus mark the natural, or structurally inevitable, evolutionary development of human existence from ordinary egoic birth to the ultimate stages of God-Realization. In the Way of Radical Understanding, which is the Way that Master Da Free John Teaches, the Awakened disposition of the seventh stage is made the foundation of life and spiritual practice through each individual's cultivation of Communion with the Divine via Master Da Free John. Thus, in this Way all growth and evolution are relieved of the dilemmas of un-Happiness, seeking, and the illusions that characterize the first six stages of life when lived apart from the instruction and Transmission of a seventh stage Adept.

About The Johannine Daist Communion

The spiritual fellowship of practitioners of the Way Taught by Master Da Free John is called THE JOHANNINE DAIST COMMUNION. "Johannine" means "having the character of John," which means "one through whom God is Gracious." "Da" is a title of respect and an indication of spiritual stature and function, meaning "one who Gives or Transmits the Divine Influence and Awakening to living beings."

The Communion has four divisions:

THE LAUGHING MAN INSTITUTE, which is the public education division and the educational and cultural organization for beginning practitioners.

THE FREE COMMUNION CHURCH, which is the educational and cultural organization for maturing practitioners.

THE ADVAITAYANA BUDDHIST ORDER, which is reserved for those in the advanced stages of practice.

THE CRAZY WISDOM FELLOWSHIP, which consists of devotees who have Realized the ultimate stage of practice of the Way.

An Invitation

If you would like to know more about the study and practice of the Spiritual Teaching of Master Da Free John or about how to begin to practice the Way, please write:

THE LAUGHING MAN INSTITUTE
P.O. Box 836
San Rafael, California 94915

The Books of Master Da Free John

SOURCE TEXTS

THE KNEE OF LISTENING
The Early Life and Radical Spiritual Teachings of Bubba [Da] Free John
$7.95 paper

THE METHOD OF THE SIDDHAS
Talks with Bubba [Da] Free John on the Spiritual Technique of the Saviors of Mankind
$8.95 paper

THE HYMN OF THE MASTER
A Confessional Recitation on the Mystery of the Spiritual Master based on the principal verses of the Guru Gita *(freely selected, rendered, and adapted)*
$8.95 paper

THE FOUR FUNDAMENTAL QUESTIONS
Talks and essays about human experience and the actual practice of an Enlightened Way of Life
$1.95 paper

THE LIBERATOR (ELEUTHERIOS)
A summation of the radical process of Enlightenment, or God-Realization, taught by the "Western Adept," Master Da Free John
$12.95 cloth, $6.95 paper

THE ENLIGHTENMENT OF THE WHOLE BODY
A Rational and New Prophetic Revelation of the Truth of Religion, Esoteric Spirituality, and the Divine Destiny of Man
$14.95 paper

SCIENTIFIC PROOF OF THE EXISTENCE OF GOD WILL SOON BE ANNOUNCED BY THE WHITE HOUSE!
Prophetic Wisdom about the Myths and Idols of mass culture and popular religious cultism, the new priesthood of scientific and political materialism, and the secrets of Enlightenment hidden in the body of Man
$12.95 paper

THE PARADOX OF INSTRUCTION
An Introduction to the Esoteric Spiritual Teaching of Bubba [Da] Free John
$14.95 cloth, $8.95 paper

NIRVANASARA
Radical Transcendentalism and the Introduction of Advaitayana Buddhism
$9.95 paper

INSPIRATIONAL AND DEVOTIONAL TEXTS

CRAZY DA MUST SING, INCLINED TO HIS WEAKER SIDE
Confessional Poems of Liberation and Love
$6.95 paper

FOREHEAD, BREATH, AND SMILE
An Anthology of Devotional Readings from the Spiritual Teaching of Master Da Free John
$20.95 cloth

OPEN EYES
A Tribute to Master Da Free John on the Tenth Commemorative Celebration of the World-Proclamation of the Way of Radical Understanding
$44.95 cloth, $25.00 paper

REMEMBRANCE OF THE DIVINE NAMES OF DA
One Hundred Eight Names of the Divine Reality and the Radiant Adept Master Da Free John
by Georg and Pat Feuerstein
$4.95 paper

MANUALS OF PRACTICE

THE FIRE GOSPEL
Essays and Talks on Spiritual Baptism
$8.95 paper

COMPULSORY DANCING
Talks and Essays on the spiritual and evolutionary necessity of emotional surrender to the Life-Principle
$3.95 paper

THE WAY THAT I TEACH
Talks on the Intuition of Eternal Life
$14.95 cloth, $9.95 paper

THE YOGA OF CONSIDERATION AND THE WAY THAT I TEACH
Talks and Essays on the distinction between preliminary practices and the radical Way of prior Enlightenment
$7.95 paper

THE DREADED GOM-BOO, OR THE IMAGINARY DISEASE THAT RELIGION SEEKS TO CURE
A Collection of Essays and Talks on the "Direct" Process of Enlightenment Taught by Master Da Free John
$9.95 paper

BODILY WORSHIP OF THE LIVING GOD
The Esoteric Practice of Prayer Taught by Da Free John
$10.95 paper

THE BODILY SACRIFICE OF ATTENTION
Introductory Talks on Radical Understanding and the Life of Divine Ignorance
$10.95 paper

"I" IS THE BODY OF LIFE
Talks and Essays on the Art and Science of Equanimity and the Self-Transcending Process of Radical Understanding
$10.95 paper

THE BODILY LOCATION OF HAPPINESS
On the Incarnation of the Divine Person and the Transmission of Love-Bliss
$8.95 paper

THE GOD IN EVERY BODY BOOK
Talks and Essays on God-Realization
$3.95 paper

PRACTICAL TEXTS

EASY DEATH
Talks and Essays on the Inherent and Ultimate Transcendence of Death and Everything Else
$10.95 paper

CONSCIOUS EXERCISE AND THE TRANSCENDENTAL SUN
The principle of love applied to exercise and the method of common physical action. A science of whole body wisdom, or true emotion, intended most especially for those engaged in religious or spiritual life.
$10.95 cloth, $8.95 paper

THE EATING GORILLA COMES IN PEACE
The Transcendental Principle of Life Applied to Diet and the Regenerative Discipline of True Health
$12.95 paper

RAW GORILLA
The Principles of Regenerative Raw Diet Applied in True Spiritual Practice
$3.95 paper

LOVE OF THE TWO-ARMED FORM
The Free and Regenerative Function of Sexuality in Ordinary Life, and the Transcendence of Sexuality in True Religious or Spiritual Practice
$12.95 paper

PAMPHLETS

THE TRANSCENDENCE OF EGO AND EGOIC SOCIETY
$1.50 paper

A CALL FOR THE RADICAL REFORMATION OF CHRISTIANITY
$2.00 paper

FOR CHILDREN

WHAT TO REMEMBER TO BE HAPPY
A Spiritual Way of Life for Your First Fourteen Years or So
$3.95 paper

I AM HAPPINESS
A Rendering for Children of the Spiritual Adventure of Master Da Free John
Adapted by Daji Bodha and Lynne Closser from
The Knee of Listening *by Da Free John*
$8.95 paper

PERIODICALS

CRAZY WISDOM
The Monthly Journal of The Johannine Daist Communion
12 copies $36.00

THE LAUGHING MAN
The Alternative to Scientific Materialism and Religious Provincialism
4 copies (quarterly) $14.00

CASSETTE TAPES

UNDERSTANDING
A consideration by Da Free John
$9.95 cassette

THE FOUNDATION AND THE SOURCE
A consideration by Da Free John
$9.95 cassette

THE YOGA OF CONSIDERATION AND THE WAY THAT I TEACH
A consideration by Da Free John
$9.95 cassette

THE BODILY LOCATION OF HAPPINESS
A talk by Da Free John
$9.95 cassette

CRAZY DA MUST SING, INCLINED TO HIS WEAKER SIDE
Da Free John reads his Confessional Poems of Liberation and Love
$9.95 cassette

FEEL THE MYSTERY
A guided meditation for children based on instructions by Da Free John
$7.95 cassette

DA BELLS
Tibetan "singing bowls" played by Da Free John
$8.95 cassette

HEAR MY BREATHING HEART
Songs of Invocation and Praise Inspired by the Teaching and Presence of Da Free John by The First Amendment Choir
$8.95 Dolby stereo

TRUTH IS THE ONLY PROFOUND
Devotional readings from the Teaching of Da Free John set to a background of devotional music and songs
$9.95 cassette

THE TRANSCENDENCE OF FAMILIARITY
A consideration by Da Free John
$9.95 cassette

A BIRTHDAY MESSAGE FROM JESUS AND ME
A talk by Da Free John
$9.95 cassette

THE PRESUMPTION OF BEING
A consideration by Da Free John
$9.95 cassette

THE GOSPEL OF THE SIDDHAS
A talk by Da Free John
$9.95 cassette

THE COSMIC MANDALA
A talk by Da Free John
$9.95 cassette

THE ULTIMATE WISDOM OF THE PERFECT PRACTICE
A consideration by Da Free John
$9.95 cassette

THE HYMN OF THE MASTER
A confessional recitation of Da Free John's The Hymn of the Master
by a devotee
$7.95 cassette

VIDEOTAPE

THE BODILY LOCATION OF HAPPINESS
A consideration by Da Free John
$108, 54 minutes, VHS format

Classic Spiritual Literature

THE SECRET GOSPEL
The Discovery and Interpretation of the Secret Gospel According to Mark
by Morton Smith
$7.95 paper

LONG PILGRIMAGE
The Life and Teaching of The Shivapuri Baba
by John G. Bennett
$7.95 paper

THE DIVINE MADMAN
The Sublime Life and Songs of Drukpa Kunley
translated by Keith Dowman
$7.95 paper

THE YOGA OF LIGHT
The Classic Esoteric Handbook of Kundalini Yoga
by Hans-Ulrich Rieker,
translated by Elsy Becherer
$7.95 paper

A NEW APPROACH TO BUDDHISM
by Dhiravamsa
$3.95 paper

VEDANTA AND CHRISTIAN FAITH
by Bede Griffiths
$3.95 paper

FOUNDING THE LIFE DIVINE
by Morwenna Donnelly
$7.95 paper

BREATH, SLEEP, THE HEART, AND LIFE
The Revolutionary Health Yoga of Pundit Acharya
$7.95 paper

THE SPIRITUAL INSTRUCTIONS OF SAINT SERAPHIM OF SAROV
edited and with an introduction by Da Free John
$3.95 paper

THE SONG OF THE SELF SUPREME
Aṣṭāvakra Gītā
Preface by Da Free John
translated by Radhakamal Mukerjee
$9.95 paper

The books of Da Free John are available at fine bookstores or by mail order from:

> **THE DAWN HORSE BOOK DEPOT**
> P.O. Box 3680, Dept. A
> Clearlake, CA 95422

Add $1.25 for the first book or tape and $.35 for each additional book or tape. California residents add 6% sales tax.